Barcelona

DIRECTIONS

CARRER
DE
SANTA ANNA

WRITTEN AND RESEARCHED BY

Jules Brown

ROUGH
GUIDES

NEW YORK • LONDON • DELHI

www.roughguides.com

Contents

Introduction to

Barcelona

It's tempting to say that there's nowhere quite like Barcelona – there's certainly not another city in Spain to touch it for sheer style, looks or energy. The glossy mags and travel press dwell enthusiastically on its outrageous architecture, designer shopping, hip bars and vibrant cultural scene, but Barcelona is more than just this year's fad. It's a confident, progressive city, one that is tirelessly self-renewing while preserving all that's best about its past.

▲ Palau Güell

The province of Catalunya (Catalonia in English), of which Barcelona is the capital, has a historical identity going back as far as the ninth century, and through the long period of domination by outside powers, as well as during the Franco dictatorship, it proved impossible to stifle the Catalan spirit. The city reflects this independence, being at the forefront of Spanish political activism, radical design and architecture, and commercial dynamism.

When to visit

The best times to go to Barcelona are late **spring** and early **autumn**, when the weather is still comfortably warm, around 21–25°C, and walking the streets isn't a chore. In **summer**, the city can be unbearably hot and humid with temperatures averaging 28°C (but often a lot more). August sees the climate at its most unwelcoming, while many shops, bars and restaurants close as local inhabitants head out of the city in droves. It's worth considering a **winter** break, as long as you don't mind the prospect of occasional rain. It's generally still warm enough to sit out at a café, even in December when the temperature hovers around 13°C.

This is seen most perfectly in the glorious *modernista* (Art Nouveau) buildings that stud the city's streets and avenues. Antoni Gaudí is the most famous of those who have left their mark on Barcelona in this way: his Sagrada Família church is rightly revered, but just as fascinating are the (literally) fantastic houses, apartment buildings and parks that he and his contemporaries designed.

The city also boasts a medieval old town – full of pivotal buildings from an earlier age of expansion – and a stupendous artistic legacy, from national (ie, Catalan) collections of Romanesque, Gothic and contemporary art to major galleries containing the life's work of the Catalan artists Joan Miró and Antoni Tàpies (not to mention a celebrated showcase of the work of Pablo Picasso).

Barcelona is a surprisingly easy place to find your way around, with the greater city, in effect, a series of self-contained neighbourhoods stretching out from the harbour, flanked by a brace of parks and girdled by the wooded Collserola mountains.

◀ Plaça del Pi

You could see most of the major sights in a long weekend, though it pays to get off the beaten track when you can. Designer boutiques in gentrified old-town quarters, street opera singers belting out an aria, bargain lunches in workers' taverns, neighbourhood funicular rides, unmarked gourmet restaurants, craft outlets and workshops, restored medieval palaces, suburban walks and specialist galleries – all are just as much Barcelona as the Ramblas or Gaudí's Sagrada Família.

◀ Hanging hams

Barcelona
AT A GLANCE

THE RAMBLAS

One of the city's most famous sights, the kilometre-long tree-lined avenue, filled with pedestrians, pavement cafés and performance artists, is the hub of any visit.

BARRI GÒTIC

The Gothic Quarter is the medieval nucleus of the city – a labyrinth of twisting streets and historic buildings, including La Seu (the cathedral) and the palaces and museums around Plaça del Rei.

▲ Barri Gòtic

LA RIBERA

The easternmost old-town neigh-bourhood, home to the Picasso museum, is also a fashionable boutique-and-bar destination.

▲ La Ribera

EL RAVAL

Still on the cusp between edgi-ness and artiness, this western old-town neighbourhood contains both the flagship museum of con-temporary art and the pick of the latest designer shops, bars and restaurants.

PORT VELL

The spruced-up Old Port harbour area features high-profile visitor attractions like the aquarium and Maremàgnum retail-and-leisure centre.

▲ Port Vell

▲ Barceloneta

BARCELONETA

The former fishing quarter beyond Port Vell boasts the city's most concentrated batch of seafood restaurants, and marks the start of a series of beaches running up past the Port Olímpic.

◄ Castel de Montjuïc

MONTJUÏC

Barcelona's best art museums and gardens, and the main Olympic stadium, are sited on the fortress-topped hill to the south-west of the centre.

EIXAMPLE

The gridded nineteenth-century uptown district contains some of Europe's most extraordinary architecture – including Gaudí's Sagrada Família.

▲ Casa Batlló, Eixample

GRÀCIA

The nicest of the suburbs on the northern edge of the city centre is a noted nightlife destination, with some offbeat bars, independent cinemas and great restaurants contained within its charming streets and squares.

Ideas

The big six

Gaudí's greatest fantasies to Picasso's earliest works, Gothic towers to Romanesque frescoes, ceramic dragons to human statues – Barcelona's must-see attractions glory in their extraordinary diversity. All are easily experienced in a long weekend, and with no charge to see three of them there's no excuse for missing out on the city's weird and wonderful highlights.

▼ Sagrada Família

If there's a more famous unfinished church in the world, Barcelona would like to know about it – the temple dedicated to the "Sacred Family" is the essential pilgrimage for Gaudí fans.

P.133 ▸ SAGRADA FAMÍLIA AND GLÒRIES

▼ Museu Picasso

Trace the genesis of the artist's genius in the city that Picasso liked to call home.

P.93 ▸ LA RIBERA AND SANT PERE

▲ The Ramblas

The city's iconic central thoroughfare is the setting for one of Europe's greatest free shows, as buskers, stall-holders, hawkers, eccentrics, locals and tourists collide to gleeful effect.

P.51 ▶ ALONG THE RAMBLAS

▲ Museu Nacional d'Art de Catalunya (MNAC)

The National Museum of Art celebrates the grandeur of Romanesque and Gothic art, two periods in which Catalunya's artists were pre-eminent in Spain.

P.109 ▶ MONTJUÏC

▼ Parc Güell

Gaudí's most playful instincts assert themselves in Barcelona's unrivalled public park, where contorted stone pavilions, gingerbread buildings and surreal ceramics combine unforgettably.

P.147 ▶ GRÀCIA AND PARC GÜELL

▼ La Seu

The city's majestic Gothic cathedral anchors the old town, with visits concentrating on the lush palm-filled cloister and marvellous roof terrace.

P.59 ▶ BARRI GÒTIC

Children's Barcelona

There's plenty for children to do, much of it free (for under 4s) or inexpensive (for under 12s). The main problem is transport, as most metro stations (except on line 2) have stairs or escalators – adults often face a stiff climb with the pushchair. Disposable nappies, baby food and formula milk are widely available in pharmacies and supermarkets, though baby-changing areas are rare, except in department stores and shopping centres.

▲ **Plaça de Vicenç Martorell**

While children play in the traffic-free square's playground, parents can rest up at the excellent café.

P.83 ▸ EL RAVAL

▲ **L'Aquàrium**

Come face to face with sharks and other sea creatures in Port Vell's highest profile (and highest-priced) all-weather family attraction.

P.75 ▸ PORT VELL AND BARCELONETA

▼ Parc d'Atraccions

On the heights of Tibidabo, overlooking the city, this terrific amusement park mixes old-fashioned rides with high-tech experiences.

P.160 ▸ TIBIDABO AND PARC DEL COLLSEROLA

▼ Font Màgica

The lights and music cut in on cue several nights a week at Montjuïc's longstanding sound-and-light show – one for all the family.

P.106 ▸ MONTJUÏC

▲ Parc Zoològic

Dolphins to big cats, Barcelona's zoo packs the world's fauna into the rolling grounds of the city's nicest park.

P.104 ▸ PARC DE LA CIUTADELLA

▲ Poble Espanyol

See Spain in a day in the "Spanish Village", an outdoor museum of reconstructed buildings, artisans' workshops and cafés that makes a great family day out.

P.108 ▸ MONTJUÏC

Stay in style

As befits Spain's style and design capital, Barcelona has a wide array of chic hotels to suit the most fashionable visitor. Rooms in the city's most elegant hotels start at about €250 a night, and it's essential to book well in advance as Barcelona doesn't really have an off-season – though prices do come down sometimes in August or at weekends, even in the top-rated establishments.

▼ Neri

This dramatic renovation of an old town palace makes a stylish base in the Barri Gòtic.

P.179 ▸ ACCOMMODATION

▼ Arts Barcelona

A beachfront beauty with the designer touch, five-star comforts and a terrific pool – this is widely considered to be Barcelona's top hotel.

P.181 ▶ ACCOMMODATION

▲ Prestige

Minimalism rules in the hotel of choice for the music and fashion world.

P.183 ▶ ACCOMMODATION

▼ Claris

Rooftop pool, beautiful rooms, and talked-about restaurant and bar, right in the heart of the modern city.

P.181 ▶ ACCOMMODATION

▲ Grand Marina

Contemporary Catalan artists have personalised this luxury waterfront hotel in Port Vell.

P.179 ▶ ACCOMMODATION

On the move

Most of Barcelona's old-town areas are only accessible on foot, but for outlying sights you can let public transport take the strain. In fact, just reaching Montjuïc and Montserrat is more than half the fun, as you have to rely on cable cars and funicular railways to climb the steep gradients. Reaching Tibidabo is even more of an adventure, with train, tram and funicular all required before getting to the top.

▲ Trasbordador Aeri

The cross-harbour cable car is an iconic Barcelona ride, but wait for a clear day for the best views.

P.78 ▶ PORT VELL AND BARCELONETA

▲ Las Golondrinas

To appreciate Barcelona the maritime city, jump on one of the daily sightseeing boats that depart from near the Columbus monument.

P.190 ▶ ESSENTIALS

▲ Telefèric de Montjuïc

This is the speediest way to the castle ramparts, and the little gondolas offer some of the best views of the city.

P.113 ▸ MONTJUÏC

▲ Cremellera de Montserrat

The towering heights of Montserrat, an hour from Barcelona, can be reached by rack railway as well as by cable car – a dramatic ride in any weather.

P.164 ▸ MONTSERRAT

▼ Tramvia Blau

It's worth trying to coincide with the antique tram service that forms part of the approach to Tibidabo.

P.160 ▸ TIBIDABO AND PARC
DEL COLLSEROLA

▼ Sightseeing tour buses

Barcelona's tour buses loop around the city stopping at every major sight and attraction – the ticket lets you jump on and off when you like.

P.190 ▸ ESSENTIALS

Festive Barcelona

Traditionally, each neighbourhood celebrates with its own festival, though the major ones – like Gràcia's Festa Major (August) and the Mercè (September) – have become city institutions. There is always a parade (often with grotesque giant figures with papier-maché heads) with music and dancing, while traditional Catalan celebrations are characterized by the *correfoc* ("fire-running"), where drummers, dragons and devils cavort in the streets, and by the *castellers*, the red-shirted human tower-builders.

▼ Dia de Sant Jordi

April 23 is St George's Day, dedicated to Catalunya's patron saint, though it's not so much dragon-slaying as book- and rose-buying that occupies the local population.

P.65 ▸ BARRI GÒTIC

▼ Festival del Grec

The summer's foremost arts and music festival centres its performances on Montjuïc's open-air Greek theatre.

P.110 ▸ MONTJUÏC

▲ Sónar

The electronic music and multimedia art world parties hard every June as Barcelona turns techno.

P.191 ▸ ESSENTIALS

▲ Festa Major de Gràcia

Competing teams of human tower-builders draw crowds at every traditional festival, piling person upon person in old-town squares in the Barri Gòtic and Gràcia – the latter's Festa Major in August is always a hoot

P.191 ▸ ESSENTIALS

▼ Festa de la Mercè

The city's biggest annual festival is dedicated to merrymaking and mayhem on a lavish scale.

P.191 ▸ ESSENTIALS

▼ Fira de Santa Llúcia

The first three weeks in December is devoted to the annual Christmas fair, held in front of La Seu.

P.191 ▸ ESSENTIALS

Shops and markets

Barcelona is great for shopping, especially for designer clothes, handcrafted accessories or stylish household items. The sharpest designers congregate in the Eixample and La Ribera; the secondhand/vintage and independent music scene focuses on El Raval, while it's the Barri Gòtic for antiques and gifts. Opening hours are Monday to Saturday 10am to 1.30/2pm, 4.30 to 7.30/8pm, though department stores and malls open until 10pm, while smaller shops vary their hours considerably.

▲ Mercat de la Boqueria

The city's finest food market is a show in its own right, busy with locals and tourists from dawn to dusk.

P.54 ▸ ALONG THE RAMBLAS

▲ Vinçon

This renowned uptown furniture and design store is a mainstay of the Barcelona shopping scene.

P.127 ▸ DRETA DE L'EIXAMPLE

▼ Traditional ceramics

Catalan and Spanish ceramics make a good gift or souvenir – Art Escudellers always has an excellent selection.

P.67 ▸ BARRI GÒTIC

▲ Designer fashion

Some of the hottest European designers call Barcelona home – check out the hip boutiques and funky shoe shops in La Ribera.

P.96 ▸ LA RIBERA AND SANT PERE

▼ Els Encants

Haggle hard and pick up a bargain at the city's biggest flea market, held every Monday, Wednesday, Friday and Saturday.

P.137 ▸ SAGRADA FAMÍLIA AND GLÒRIES

▲ Book and coin market

Join the crowds on Sunday morning at the Mercat de Sant Antoni, good fun whether you're browsing or buying.

P.85 ▸ EL RAVAL

Parks and gardens

It's not hard to find a bit of traffic-free space in Barcelona, from a quiet neighbourhood corner to a formal park. Some places, like Parc Güell and Parc de la Ciutadella, will be high on any visiting list, but to escape the crowds try hiking in the Collserola hills, just a fifteen-minute train ride away. Nearly all outdoor spaces have a kiosk-café, and many have a children's play area.

▼ Parc Güell

The city's most extraordinary park, festooned with ceramic decoration, is the product of architect Antoni Gaudí's surreal flight of fancy.

P.147 ▸ GRÀCIA AND PARC GÜELL

▼ Parc del Collserola

On the hottest of days a welcome breeze and pine-shaded springs reward hikers in the wooded hills above Barcelona.

P.162 ▸ TIBIDABO AND PARC DEL COLLSEROLA

▲ Parc de la Ciutadella

The park at the eastern edge of the old town is packed full of surprises, from palmhouse café to zoological museum.

P.102 ▸ PARC DE LA CIUTADELLA

▲ Jardí Botànic de Barcelona

Roam the various zones of Barcelona's botanical garden, or join a guided tour for a more in-depth exploration.

P.114 ▸ MONTJUÏC

▼ Parc Joan Miró

An urban park whose concrete piazza and towering Miró sculpture are tempered by a shaded garden with children's playground.

P.142 ▸ ESQUERRA DE L'EIXAMPLE

▼ Jardins de Mossèn Costa i Llobera

The huge cactus stands on the slopes of Montjuïc are a local secret, best enjoyed as the day's shadows lengthen.

P.113 ▸ MONTJUÏC

The modernista trail

Barcelona's presiding architectural genius, Antoni Gaudí i Cornet, changed the way people looked at urban architecture and, with his *modernista* contemporaries – notably Josep Puig i Cadafalch and Lluís Domènech i Montaner – also changed the way Barcelona looked. Their style, a sort of Catalan Art Nouveau, erupted in the 1870s and 1880s, and following the *modernista* trail around the city shows you some of Europe's most extraordinary buildings.

▲ La Pedrera

The "stone quarry" is the most eye-catching apartment building in the city, a sinuous structure with a fantasy roof terrace that hosts summer cocktail evenings.

P.126 ▶ DRETA DE L'EIXAMPLE

▼ Hotel España

Some of the greatest *modernista* names came together to decorate this solid old nineteenth-century hotel, which has a particularly splendid dining room.

P.84 ▸ EL RAVAL

▲ Hospital de la Santa Creu i de Sant Pau

Weekend tours show visitors the ornate buildings and pavilions of the city's most innovative public hospital.

P.136 ▸ SAGRADA FAMÍLIA AND GLÒRIES

▼ Casa Amatller

Headquarters of the Centre del Modernisme, and the best place to find out more about Barcelona's peculiar architecture.

P.124 ▸ DRETA DE L'EIXAMPLE

▲ Casa Batlló

Gaudí's Casa Batlló anchors the famous Mansana de la Discòrdia, or "Block of Discord", a trio of elaborate mansions built for the city's nineteenth-century industrialists.

P.125 ▸ DRETA DE L'EIXAMPLE

Sports and recreation

A spin-off from the 1992 Olympics was an increased provision of sports and leisure facilities throughout Barcelona. The city beaches and swimming pools draw big summer crowds, while you can rent anything from roller blades to mountain bikes to explore the back streets and promenades. However, ask a Catalan to recommend a spectator sport and there will be only one answer – football, as practised by the local heroes of FC Barcelona.

▼ Camp Nou

The city's premier team, FC Barcelona, plays in one of Europe's most magnificent stadia – if you can't get a ticket, the big game's always on TV.

P.152 ▶ CAMP NOU, PEDRALBES AND SARRIÀ-SANT GERVASI

▼ Watersports

It's easy to rent all the equipment you need for a surf or sail from the Port Olímpic.

P.117 ▶ PORT OLÍMPIC AND POBLE NOU

▲ Rent a bike

With more than 100km of cycle paths, plus beach promenades and forest trails, renting a bike offers a different way to see the city.

P.192 ▶ ESSENTIALS

▲ Passeig Marítim

Early mornings and weekends are the best times to work out on the harbourside promenade between Barceloneta and the Port Olímpic.

P.77 ▶ PORT VELL AND
BARCELONETA

▼ Estadi Olímpic

The Olympic Stadium, remodelled for the 1992 Games, is at the heart of an Olympic area that includes world-class swimming and sports facilities.

P.111 ▶ MONTJUÏC

▼ City beaches

When the gallery-going, shopping and bar-hopping flags, spend the day at the beach – Barcelona has five kilometres of sand-fringed ocean.

P.119 ▶ PORT OLÍMPIC AND
POBLE NOU

Historic Barcelona

Any walk around the old town provides reminders of Barcelona's long history, with a street layout and surviving walls that go back to Roman times. But it's the fourteenth- and fifteenth-century Golden Age that lent the city its Catalan-Gothic lustre, when newly built churches, city hall, government palace and shipyards all testified to Barcelona's influence. Later, the eighteenth-century Bourbons reshaped the city again, building fortresses to subdue the unruly inhabitants.

▲ Església de Sant Pau del Camp

The city's oldest church, dating from the tenth century, provides a peaceful retreat in the modern Raval.

P.85 ▸ EL RAVAL

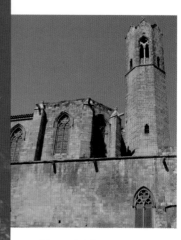

▲ Plaça del Rei

The Renaissance tower and Gothic buildings of Plaça del Rei form one of the most harmonious ensembles in the old town.

P.62 ▸ BARRI GÒTIC

▼ Monestir de Pedralbes

Half an hour from the centre lies the
Pedralbes monastery, boasting not only the
city's most harmonious cloister but also a
world-class art collection.

P.156 ▶ CAMP NOU, PEDRALBES
AND SARRIÀ-SANT GERVASI

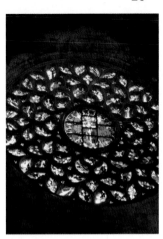

▲ Església de Santa María del Mar

Santa María was built in the roaring 1320s,
with economic confidence at its height,
making it the crowning glory of the Catalan-
Gothic style of architecture.

P.92 ▶ LA RIBERA AND SANT
PERE

▼ Museu Marítim

The engaging Maritime Museum is housed
in the great medieval shipyards that under-
pinned Barcelona's early prosperity.

P.74 ▶ PORT VELL AND
BARCELONETA

▲ Castell de Montjuïc

The hilltop Bourbon fortress offers an
eagle's-eye view of the city.

P.113 ▶ MONTJUÏC

Cafés

There are thousands of cafés, ranging from century-old coffee houses to unique neighbourhood haunts. Specialist places include a *forn* (bakery), *patisseria* (pastry shop) and *xocolateria* (specializes in chocolate), while a *granja* is more of a milk bar than a regular café, offering traditional delights like *orxata* (tiger-nut drink) and *granissat* (flavoured crushed ice). A café breakfast is typically a *flauta* (thin baguette sandwich), *ensaimada* (pastry spiral) or croissant.

▼ Zurich

"Meet me at the Zurich" is an age-old Barcelona refrain.

P.57 ▶ ALONG THE RAMBLAS

▼ Café de l'Opera

House café for the opera house opposite, this is the most traditional of the city's watering holes.

P.57 ▶ ALONG THE RAMBLAS

▲ Meson del Café

As quirky as it's small, the "House of Coffee" serves the cup that revives.

P.68 ▶ BARRI GÒTIC

▼ Laie Llibreria Café

Stop for breakfast, lunch or a read of the papers at Barcelona's best bookshop café.

P.130 ▶ DRETA DE L'EIXAMPLE

▼ Forn de Sant Jaume

This place serves some delectable cakes and pastries, to eat in or take away.

P.130 ▶ DRETA DE L'EIXAMPLE

▲ Textil Café

A relaxing museum café that's known for its good food.

P.97 ▶ LA RIBERA AND SANT PERE

Specialist museums

A selection of specialist collections adds to the city's extraordinary diversity. There are dedicated museums to the history of chocolate and the world of textiles, while other collections zero in local matters like Barcelona's football team or the nuances of Catalan history. Only the unclassifiable Museu Frederic Marès is essential viewing, but visit one or two others to unpeel a layer of the city you might otherwise have missed.

▲ Museu de la Xocolata

Handcrafted chocolates, made on the premises, are the twist at this informative museum.

P.93 ▶ LA RIBERA AND SANT PERE

▲ Museu del Futbol

No football fan will want to miss a visit to the FC Barcelona museum, presenting a wealth of trophies, photographs, videos and memorabilia.

P.153 ▶ CAMP NOU, PEDRALBES AND SARRIÀ-SANT GERVASI

▼ Museu Frederic Marès

The "mad collector" to beat them all – don't miss Marès' extraordinary range of folkloric items, household utensils, toys and ephemera, contained within a lovely old-town palace with celebrated summer café.

P.63 ▸ BARRI GÒTIC

▼ Museu de Ceràmica

The city's most comprehensive collection of ceramics is housed in one wing of a former royal palace.

P.153 ▸ CAMP NOU, PEDRALBES
          AND SARRIÀ-SANT GERVASI

▲ Museu Textil i d'Indumentaria

Textiles and clothing from Roman times to the present day illuminate one of the city's best-presented museums.

P.94 ▸ LA RIBERA AND SANT
         PERE

▲ Museu d'Història de Catalunya

An engaging presentation of all things Catalan, from the history of the national flag to Barcelona at war.

P.76 ▸ PORT VELL AND
        BARCELONETA

On the waterfront

Dramatic changes over the last two decades have once again placed harbour and Mediterranean at the heart of Barcelona. The old docksides have been opened up as promenades and entertainment areas, and the city's once grimy beaches landscaped and prettified – it's as if a theatre curtain has been lifted to reveal that, all along, Barcelona had an urban waterfront of which it could be proud.

▼ Mirador de Colón

Take the elevator up to the viewing platform of the Christopher Columbus monument to survey the ever-developing waterfront.

P.73 ▶ PORT VELL AND BARCELONETA

▼ Port Vell

The "Old Port" area at the foot of the Ramblas has seen its former warehouses and cargo wharves transformed into a vibrant entertainment zone.

P.73 ▶ PORT VELL AND BARCELONETA

▼ Barceloneta's restaurants

The Passeig de Joan Borbó promenade, in the old fishing quarter of Barceloneta, is the perfect place for a paella or seafood meal.

P.78 ▶ PORT VELL AND
BARCELONETA

▲ Luz de Gas

The floating bar (open summer only) is the best vantage-point for the comings and goings on the Port Vell promenade.

P.80 ▶ PORT VELL AND
BARCELONETA

▼ Santa Eulàlia

Step back to the days of sail with a tour of this historic schooner.

P.74 ▶ PORT VELL AND
BARCELONETA

▲ Port Olímpic

The twin towers and packed marina dominate the Port Olímpic, whose restaurants and bars make it the city's liveliest resort area.

P.117 ▶ PORT OLÍMPIC AND
POBLE NOU

Out for lunch

Restaurants generally offer a lunchtime *menú del dia* (menu of the day), starting at about €7, rising to €10/12 in fancier places or at weekends. It's a real bargain, as dinner in the same restaurant might cost three times as much. Budget places often don't have a written menu, with the waiter simply reeling off the day's dishes. Lunch hours are 1–4pm, though locals don't eat until 2pm or later.

▲ Café de l'Acadèmia
Many visitors' favourite old-town restaurant has a lovely terrace and offers up a set-price lunch that mixes contemporary and traditional Catalan flavours.

P.69 ▸ BARRI GÒTIC

▼ Agua

This is the best place on the boardwalk for a beachside lunch full of Mediterranean flavours.

P.120 ▶ PORT OLÍMPIC AND POBLE NOU

▼ Glop

A bustling Gràcia tavern is the favoured venue for a family lunch, especially at weekends when every table is occupied.

P.149 ▶ GRÀCIA AND PARC GÜELL

▲ L'Econòmic

Diners cram into this traditionally tiled lunch-only restaurant for excellent bargain meals, served Monday to Friday.

P.99 ▶ LA RIBERA AND SANT PERE

▲ Silenus

A fashionable place in the arty upper Raval for cutting-edge Barcelona cuisine.

P.89 ▶ EL RAVAL

Galleries and artists

Barcelona has the world's finest collections of work by Catalan artists Joan Miró and Antoni Tàpies, while contemporary art of all kinds anchors the displays at MACBA and Caixa Forum. The Articket (€15) gives half-price admission into all (plus others) except Caixa Forum, entry to which is free. The city also has dozens of private galleries, concentrated in La Ribera, El Raval and the Eixample – check *Guía del Ocio*'s "Arte" section for listings.

▼ Caixa Forum

There's always a show worth seeing in the city's premier arts and cultural centre – not to mention concerts, films, poetry readings and other events.

P.107 ▸ MONTJUÏC

▲ Fundacío Antoni Tàpies

Acquaint yourself with the work of the master Catalan abstract artist, contained within a striking Eixample mansion.

P.125 ▸ DRETA DE L'EIXAMPLE

▼ Col.lecció Thyssen-Bornemisza

A select gathering of fourteenth- to eighteenth-century European art occupies a hushed wing of the Pedralbes monastery.

P.157 ▸ CAMP NOU, PEDRALBES AND SARRIÀ-SANT GERVASI

▼ Museu d'Art Contemporani de Barcelona (MACBA)

Post-war contemporary art (Spanish, Catalan and international) has a home in El Raval's signature building.

P.81 ▸ EL RAVAL

▲ Fundacío Joan Miró

There's no more beautiful gallery in the city than the house on the hill presenting the life's work of Joan Miró.

P.112 ▸ MONTJUÍC

Traditional food and drink

Traditional Catalan food doesn't stray far from its rural and maritime roots – think bread rubbed with tomato, oil and garlic, chargrilled meats and vegetables, fish stews, salt cod, sausage with haricot beans, or mixed rice dishes. Even the most fashionable restaurants present a few homestyle favourites for local diners brought up on earthy flavours and large portions. However, sophistication comes in the shape of a glass of *cava*, Catalan champagne.

▲ Bread with tomato (pa amb tomàquet)

Often topped with cured ham, sliced cheese or grilled vegetables – try it for breakfast or as an appetizer in a local restaurant like *Els Tres Tombs*.

P.89 ▶ EL RAVAL

▲ From the grill

Food cooked on the chargrill (*a la brasa*) is a staple at *Taverna La Tomaquera* – not just meats, but also seasonal artichokes and huge spring onions.

P.115 ▶ MONTJUÏC

▼ A glass of fizz

Order the house *cava* at *Xampanyet* to accompany sliced meats and cheeses or a dish of the local anchovies.

P.100 ▶ LA RIBERA AND SANT PERE

▲ Orxata

A traditional café – like *El Tio Che* – is the best place to sample the unique milky beverage made from ground tiger nuts.

P.119 ▶ PORT OLÍMPIC AND POBLE NOU

▼ Grilled sausage (botifarra)

Bar Salvador can usually oblige with a bumper serving of pork sausage served on a pool of stewed haricot beans (*mongetes*).

P.98 ▶ LA RIBERA AND SANT PERE

▲ Noodles (fideuà)

The local alternative to paella is noodles served with seafood and a fiery garlic mayonnaise – restaurants in Barceloneta all have their own version.

P.78 ▶ PORT VELL AND BARCELONETA

Music, dance and theatre

You can catch concerts, plays and performances at a wide variety of venues, and internationally renowned artists often appear in the city – particularly during the summer-long *Grec* festival or at the annual festivals devoted to ancient music (May), contemporary music (Oct/Nov) and jazz (Nov/Dec). City-sponsored productions are advertised at the Palau de la Virreina on the Ramblas (@www.bcn.es/cultura), and you can buy advance concert, theatre and show tickets from ServiCaixa (@www.servicaixa.com) or TelEntrada (@www.telentrada.com).

▼ Palau de la Música Catalana

Concerts at this extravagant *modernista*-designed concert hall are a treat, while the popular daily guided tours are an added attraction.

P.91 ▸ LA RIBERA AND SANT PERE

▼ Gran Teatre del Liceu

The renowned Liceu is a city landmark, but book ahead if you want tickets, either for a night at the opera or the late-night recitals.

P.55 ▸ ALONG THE RAMBLAS

▲ Teatre Nacional de Catalunya

The National Theatre – a remarkable modern take on a Greek temple – has a mission to promote Catalan-language productions.

P.138 ▶ SAGRADA FAMÍLIA AND GLÒRIES

▲ Tarantos

A longstanding favourite for flamenco, jazz, funk and jam sessions – the after-show dancing keeps on into the small hours.

P.72 ▶ BARRI GÒTIC

▼ Sidecar

This rootsy Plaça Reial rock club presents a varied roster of low-priced gigs and club nights.

P.72 ▶ BARRI GÒTIC

▼ L'Auditori

Barcelona's finest concert hall has a year-round programme of classical and contemporary music.

P.138 ▶ SAGRADA FAMÍLIA AND GLÒRIES

Out on the town

When it comes to a day's lazing around or a night's carousing, Barcelona offers style, tradition and kitsch in equal measures. From tapas-tasting to view-gazing, laidback café-bar to full-on techno temple, bohemian boozer to cocktail emporium – you'll find it somewhere. For the latest listings buy the weekly *Guia del Ocio* (out every Thursday), which covers bars, venues and opening hours in its "Tarde Noche" section.

▲ Rosal

Don't miss a bar crawl in the hip old-town area of the Born – Rosal is a favoured drop-in spot for planning the night's entertainment, though some don't leave until closing time.

P.97 ▸ LA RIBERA AND SANT PERE

▲ Fira

Only in Barcelona – fairground rides, pop-corn and champagne in one of the city's most unique uptown bars.

P.144 ▸ ESQUERRA DE L'EIXAMPLE

▼ Mirablau

The city does great views and great bars –
Mirablau combines both to stunning effect.

P.163 ▸ TIBIDABO AND PARC
DEL COLLSEROLA

▼ Quimet i Quimet

There's a touch of class – and seriously
good tapas – at this in-the-know bar on the
old town fringes.

P.115 ▸ MONTJUÏC

▲ Bar Ra

El Raval has a score or more of quirky
drinking haunts, none funkier or more
colourful than Bar Ra.

P.89 ▸ EL RAVAL

▲ Bosc de la Fades

There's kitsch, and then there's the "Forest
of the Fairies", the rustic grotto-bar at the
foot of the Ramblas.

P.58 ▸ ALONG THE RAMBLAS

City landmarks

By any standards Barcelona has its fair share of iconic locations and buildings, from the Ramblas to the Sagrada Família. Buildings associated with the International Exhibitions of 1888 and 1929, plus construction for the 1992 Olympics and 2004 Universal Forum, have helped to provide an extraordinary city backdrop. Meanwhile, contemporary architects have added towers, installations, squares and parks – some controversial, others much-loved landmarks – that bolster the city's reputation as an evolving urban experiment.

▼ The Frank Gehry fish

Showpiece landmark of the Port Olímpic is the enormous glittering fish that straddles the promenade.

P.117 ▶ PORT OLÍMPIC AND POBLE NOU

▼ Torre de Collserola

Norman Foster's communications tower is easily visible on the Barcelona skyline, and is just a short walk from the Tibidabo amusement park.

P.161 ▶ TIBIDABO AND PARC DEL COLLSEROLA

▲ Plaça de Catalunya

The whole city comes and goes through this pivotal square, where just-off-the-metro tourists mingle with office-workers, buskers, shoppers and café patrons.

P.51 ▶ ALONG THE RAMBLAS

▲ Maremàgnum

No visit to Port Vell is complete without a stroll along the boardwalk to the harbourside entertainment zone and shopping complex.

P.75 ▶ PORT VELL AND BARCELONETA

▼ Arc de Triomf

Barcelona's triumphant arch, relic of the 1888 Universal Exhibition, provides the gateway to the Parc de la Ciutadella area.

P.102 ▶ PARC DE LA CIUTADELLA

▼ Clocktower, Plaça Rius i Taulet

Lunch or a drink under Gràcia's landmark clocktower is always a pleasure.

P.147 ▶ GRÀCIA AND PARC GÜELL

Places

Along the Ramblas

No day in the city seems complete without a stroll along the Ramblas, Spain's most famous thoroughfare. Cutting through Barcelona's old town areas, and connecting Plaça de Catalunya with the harbour, it's at the heart of the city's life and self-image – lined with cafés, restaurants, souvenir shops, flower stalls and newspaper kiosks. The name, derived from the Arabic ramla (or "sand"), refers to the bed of a seasonal stream, which was paved over in medieval times. Decorative benches, plane trees and stately buildings were added in the nineteenth century as the Ramblas became the locals' perambulation of choice. Today, the show goes on, day or night, as street vendors, human statues, portrait painters, buskers and card sharps add to the colour and character of Barcelona's most enthralling street. There are metro stops at Catalunya (top of the Ramblas), Liceu (middle) and Drassanes (bottom), or you can walk the entire length in about twenty minutes.

Plaça de Catalunya

The huge square at the top of the Ramblas stands right at the heart of the city, with the old town and port below it, and the planned Eixample district above and beyond. It was laid out in its present form in the 1920s, centred on a formal layout of statues, fountains and trees, and is the focal point of local events and demonstrations – notably the mass gathering here on New Year's Eve. The most prominent monument is the towering angular slab and bust dedicated to Francesc Macià, first president of the Generalitat (Catalan government), who died in office in 1933. For visitors, the square is known as the site of the main city tourist office (see p.188) – down the steps in the southeastern corner – while an initial orientation point is the white-faced El Corte Inglés department store on the eastern side of the square. Across on the

▼ RAMBLAS FLOWER STALL

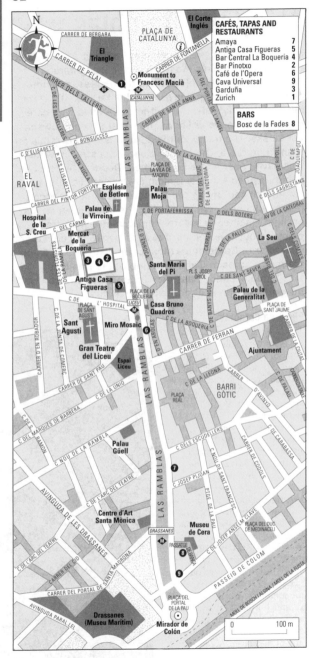

CAFÉS, TAPAS AND
RESTAURANTS
Amaya	7
Antiga Casa Figueras	5
Bar Central La Boqueria	4
Bar Pinotxo	2
Café de l'Opera	6
Cava Universal	9
Garduña	3
Zurich	1

BARS
Bosc de la Fades	8

southwest side (over the road from the top of the Ramblas) is El Triangle shopping centre, incorporating not only a variety of stores and exhibition space but also the popular *Zurich* café (p.57) in its ground floor.

▲ RAMBLAS FOUNTAIN

Església de Betlem

Ramblas 107 ☎933 183 823. Daily 8am–6pm. It seems hard to believe, but the Ramblas was a war zone during the Spanish Civil War as the city erupted into factionalism. With anarchists sacking the city's churches at will in 1936, the rich interior of the Baroque Església de Betlem (1681) was completely destroyed by fire and only the main facade on c/del Carme survived the destruction: it still sports a fine sculpted portal and a relief depicting the Nativity.

Palau Moja

Ramblas 188 ☎933 162 740. Bookshop Mon–Fri 9am–8pm, Sat 9am–2pm & 4–8pm; Sala Palau Moja Tues–Sat 11am–8pm, Sun 11am–3pm. Gallery admission usually free. The arcaded Palau Moja dates from the late eighteenth century and still retains an exterior staircase and elegant great hall. The ground floor of the building, restored by the Generalitat, is now a bookshop relating to all things Catalan, while the palace's gallery, the Sala Palau Moja, is open for contemporary art exhibitions – the gallery entrance is around the corner in c/Portaferrissa. Take a look, too, at the illustrated tiles above the fountain at the start of c/Portaferrissa, which show the medieval gate (the *Porta Ferriça*) and market that once stood here.

Palau de la Virreina

Ramblas 99 ☎933 017 775, Ⓦwww.bcn.es/cultura. Galleries Tues–Fri 11am–2pm & 4–8.30pm, Sat 11am–8.30pm, Sun 11am–3pm; information office Mon–Sat 10am–8pm, Sun 11am–3pm. The graceful eighteenth-century Palau de la Virreina is set back slightly from the Ramblas. Commissioned by a Peruvian viceroy, Manuel Amat, and named after the wife who survived him, its five Ramblas-facing bays are adorned with pilasters and Rococo windows. Today the building's galleries are used to house changing exhibitions of contemporary art and photography (admission sometimes charged). The ground floor of the palace also contains the Institut de Cultura's walk-in information centre and ticket office for cultural events run by the Ajuntament (city council). There's a shop too (Tues–Sat 10am–8.30pm), featuring locally produced objets d'art and other items relating to the city.

▼ PALAU DE LA VIRREINA

Mercat de la Boqueria

Ramblas 91 ☎ 933 182 584, ⓦ www.ac-boqueria.com. Mon–Sat 6am–8pm. The city's glorious main food market is officially called the Mercat Sant Josep, though it's referred to locally as La Boqueria. Built on the site of a former convent between 1836 and 1840, the cavernous hall stretches back behind the high wrought-iron entrance arch facing the Ramblas. It's a riot of noise and colour, as popular with locals who come here to shop daily as with snap-happy tourists. Everything radiates out from the central banks of fish and seafood stalls – great piles of fruit and vegetables, bunches of herbs and pots of spices, baskets of wild mushrooms, mounds of cheese and sausage, racks of bread, hanging hams, and meat counters dripping blood into the gutters below. If you're going to buy, do some browsing first, as the flagship fruit and veg stalls by the entrance tend to have higher prices than those further inside. There are also some excellent stand-up snack bars in here – the *Pinotxo* the most famous – and a good market restaurant (*Garduña*) at the back of the building; see p.58 for both.

Plaça de la Boqueria

The halfway point of the Ramblas is marked by Plaça de la Boqueria, which sports a large round mosaic by Joan Miró in the middle of the pavement. This is one of a number of public works in the city by the

Ramblas statues

You can't move for human statues on the Ramblas. As fads and fashions change, Greek statues and Charlie Chaplins have given way to the latest movie characters, standing immobile on their little home-made plinths, daring you to catch them out in a blink. Some join in the fun – "Mr Burns" and "Lisa Simpson" posing jauntily for photographs, "Matador" swirling a cape for the camera, "Orange Twirly Girl" windmilling her streamers as money is dropped in front of her. Many are actors (or at least waiters who say they're actors), and others make a claim to art – how else to begin to explain "Silver Cowboy", lounging on the railings at Liceu metro, or "Tree Sprite", clinging chameleon-like to one of the Ramblas plane trees. Then there's the plain weird, like "Lady Under Rock", her bottom half crushed under a boulder, issuing plaintive shrieks at passers-by.

▲ MIRÓ MOSAIC

artist, who was born just a couple of minutes' walk off the Ramblas in the Barri Gòtic. Close by, at Ramblas 82, the **Casa Bruno Quadros** – the lower floor is now the *Caixa Sabadell* – was built in the 1890s to house an umbrella store. Its unusual facade is decorated with a green dragon and Oriental designs, and scattered with parasols. On the other side of the Ramblas at no. 83, there are more *modernista* flourishes on the **Antiga Casa Figueras** (1902), which overdoses on stained glass and mosaics, and sports a corner relief of a female reaper. It's now a renowned bakery-café (see p.57).

Gran Teatre del Liceu

Ramblas 51–59 ® www.liceubarcelona
.com. Box office ⊕ 934 859 913; tours
⊕ 934 859 914, depart daily 10am,
11.30am, noon & 1pm. €3.50/5.50.
Barcelona's celebrated opera house was first founded in 1847 and rebuilt after a fire in 1861 to become Spain's grandest theatre. Regarded as a bastion of the city's late nineteenth-century commercial and intellectual classes, the Liceu was devastated again in 1893 when an anarchist threw two bombs into the stalls during a production of *William Tell* – twenty people died. The Liceu then burned down for the third time in 1994, when a worker's blowtorch set fire to the scenery during last-minute alterations to an opera set. Fully restored once more, the lavishly decorated interior is accessible on tours, which depart from the opera house's modern extension, the Espai Liceu – you'll see and learn most on the guided 10am tour (the other, cheaper tours are self-guided). If you want to attend an opera or recital (including the popular late-night concerts or *sessions golfes*), you should check the website for details and make bookings well in advance.

Centre d'Art Santa Mònica

Ramblas 7 ⊕ 933 162 810, ® http
://cultura.gencat.net/casm. Tues–Sat
11am–8pm, Sun 11am–3pm. Free. The Augustinian convent of Santa Mònica dates originally from 1626, making it the oldest building on the Ramblas. It was entirely remodelled in the 1980s, and now hosts regularly changing exhibitions of contemporary art

on the ground floor. There's also a city information office at the centre, and a café-bar upstairs. Pavement artists and palm readers occasionally set up stall outside here on the Ramblas, augmented on weekend afternoons by a small street market selling jewellery and ornaments.

Museu de Cera

Ramblas 4–6, entrance on Ptge. de Banca ☎933 172 649, ⊛www .museocerabcn.com. July–Sept daily 10am–1pm; Oct–June Mon–Fri 10am–1.30pm & 4–7.30pm, Sat & Sun 11am–2pm & 4.30–8.30pm. €6.65. The city's wax museum is located in an impressive nineteenth-century bank building. It presents the usual trawl through the internationally famous and infamous, plus dated film characters, a mixed bag of public figures from Mother Teresa to Yasser Arafat, and underwater and space capsule simulations. However, if this doesn't appeal, it is worth at least poking your head into the museum's extraordinary bar, the *Bosc de les Fades* (p.58), while for aficionados of kitsch there are night visits every Saturday at 8.30pm and 9.30pm (€12, drink included; in Spanish only) with actors and special effects ratcheting up the atmosphere.

Shops

El Corte Inglés

Pl. de Catalunya 14 ☎933 063 800, ⊛www.elcorteingles.es. The city's biggest department store has nine retail floors, a basement supermarket and – best of all – a top-floor café with terrific views.

Espai Liceu

Ramblas 51–59 ☎934 859 913. The shop and café in the opera house extension has the widest range of opera CDs and DVDs in the city, as well as selling Liceu branded T-shirts, coffee mugs, ceramics and other souvenirs.

El Triangle

Pl. de Catalunya 4 ☎933 180 108. Shopping centre dominated by the flagship FNAC store, which specializes in books (good travel and English selections), music CDs and computer software. Also a Camper (Spain's most stylish, value-for-money shoe-shop chain), Sephora for cosmetics, Habitat, and various clothes shops, plus magazines and café on the ground floor.

▼ RAMBLAS KIOSK

Cava Universal

Pl. Portal de la Pau 4 ☎933 026 184. Daily 9am–10pm. A useful drinks and snacks spot on the lower Ramblas, with a sunny *terrassa* looking directly onto the Columbus monument.

Zurich

Pl. Catalunya 1 ☎933 179 153. Mon–Fri 8am–11pm, Sat & Sun 10am–11pm, June–Sept open until 1am. The most famous meet-and-greet café in town, right at the top of the Ramblas underneath El Triangle shopping centre. It's good for croissants and breakfast *bocadillos* (sandwiches) and there's a huge terrace, but sit inside if you don't want to be bothered by endless rounds of buskers and beggars.

▲ ANTIGA CASA FIGUERAS

Cafés

Antiga Casa Figueras

Ramblas 83 ☎933 016 027. Mon–Sat 9am–3pm & 5–8.30pm. Pastries from the Escribà family business in a *modernista*-designed pastry shop, with a few tables inside and out. Many people rate this as the best bakery in Barcelona.

Café de l'Opera

Ramblas 74 ☎933 177 585. Daily 9am–3am. This venerable café-bar retains its late nineteenth-century decor as well as a bank of sought-after pavement tables. It's not a complete tourist-fest – long a favourite for pre- and post-performance refreshments, locals pop in for fine coffee, a good range of cakes, snacks and tapas, or a late-night *sangria de cava*.

Restaurants and tapas bars

Amaya

Ramblas 20–24 ☎933 026 138 (bar), ☎933 021 037 (restaurant), ✆www.restauranteamaya.com. Bar daily 10am–12.30am; restaurant daily 1.30–4pm & 8.30pm–midnight. A Ramblas fixture since 1941 – restaurant on one side, tapas bar on the other, both serving very good Basque seafood specialities, including octopus, baby squid, clams, mussels, anchovies and prawns. The smoke-filled bar offers the cheapest (and most enjoyable) introduction to the cuisine; otherwise, main dishes in the restaurant cost €14–20.

Bar Central la Boqueria

Mercat de la Boqueria, Ramblas 91; no phone. Mon–Sat 6.30am–4pm. The gleaming chrome stand-up bar in the central aisle is the venue for ultra-fresh market produce,

▲ AMAYA RESTAURANT

served by blue-smocked staff who work at a fair lick. Breakfast, snack or lunch, it's all the same to them – salmon cutlets, sardines, calamari, razor clams, hake fillets, sausages, pork steaks, asparagus spears and the rest, plunked on the griddle and sprinkled with salt. Breakfast costs just a few euros, more like €5–10 for a main dish and a drink.

Bar Pinotxo

Mercat de la Boqueria, Ramblas 91 ☎933 171 731. Mon–Sat 6am–5pm. The market's most renowned refuelling stop – just inside the main entrance on the right – attracts traders, chefs, tourists and celebs, who stand three deep at busy times. A *tallat* (small white coffee) and a grilled sandwich is the local breakfast of choice; otherwise let the cheery staff steer you towards the tapas and daily specials.

Garduña

Mercat de la Boqueria, c/Jerusalem 18 ☎933 024 323. Mon–Sat 1–4pm & 8pm–midnight. Tucked away at the back of the frenetic Boqueria market, this is a great place for lunch (when there's a €9.50 *menú del dia*; otherwise €13.50 at night) – basically, you're going to be offered the best of the day's produce at pretty reasonable prices, and if you're lucky you'll get a seat with market views.

Bars

Bosc de les Fades

Ptge. de Banca 5 ☎933 172 649. Mon–Thurs & Sun 10.30am–1am, Fri & Sat 10.30am–3am. Tucked away in an alley off the Ramblas, by the wax museum, the "Forest of the Fairies" is festooned with gnarled plaster tree trunks, hanging branches, fountains and stalactites. It's a bit cheesy, which is perhaps why it's a huge hit with the twenty-something crowd who huddle in the grottoes and decorative side rooms.

Barri Gòtic

The highly picturesque Barri Gòtic, or Gothic Quarter, on the east side of the Ramblas, forms the very heart of Barcelona's old town. Its buildings date principally from the fourteenth and fifteenth centuries, when Barcelona reached the height of her medieval prosperity, and culminate in the extraordinary Gothic cathedral known as La Seu. Fanning out from here are arcaded squares and skinny alleys containing several fascinating museums and the surviving portions of the city's Roman walls. It will take the best part of a day to see everything – more if you indulge yourself in the abundant cafés, antique shops, boutiques and galleries. The main areas to explore lie north of c/de Ferran and c/de Jaume I, around the cathedral; and south from Plaça Reial and c/d'Avinyo to the harbour – the latter district is rather less gentrified than the cathedral area and you should take care at night in the poorly lit streets. Metros Liceu and Jaume I mark the east–west boundaries of the Barri Gòtic.

▼ LA SEU

La Seu

Pl. de la Seu ☎ 933 151 554, ⓦ www.catedralbcn.org. Mon–Fri 8am–1.15pm & 5–7.30pm, Sat & Sun 8am–1.15pm & 5–7.45pm. Free.
Barcelona's cathedral is one of the great Gothic buildings of Spain. Located on a site previously occupied by a Roman temple, it was begun in 1298 and finished in 1448 – save the neo-Gothic principal facade, completed in the 1880s. La Seu is dedicated to Santa Eulàlia, who was martyred by the Romans for daring to prefer Christianity, and her ornate tomb rests in a crypt beneath the high altar. However, the most renowned part of the cathedral is its magnificent fourteenth-century **cloister** (daily 9am–1pm & 5–7pm; free), which looks over a lush tropical garden complete with soaring palm trees and honking white geese. Don't leave without ascending to the **roof**

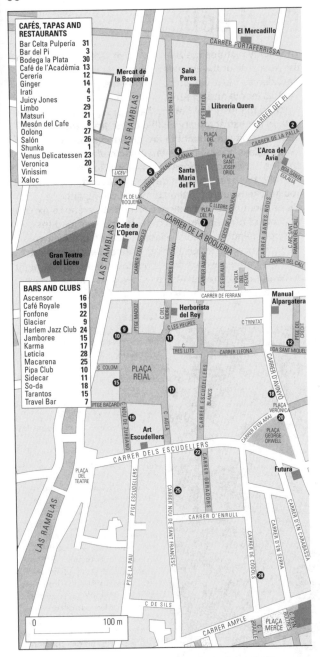

CAFÉS, TAPAS AND RESTAURANTS

Bar Celta Pulpería	31
Bar del Pi	3
Bodega la Plata	30
Café de l'Acadèmia	13
Cererîa	12
Ginger	14
Irati	4
Juicy Jones	5
Limbo	29
Matsuri	21
Mesón del Cafe	8
Oolong	27
Salón	26
Shunka	1
Venus Delicatessen	23
Veronica	20
Vinissim	6
Xaloc	2

BARS AND CLUBS

Ascensor	16
Café Royale	19
Fonfone	22
Glaciar	9
Harlem Jazz Club	24
Jamboree	15
Karma	17
Leticia	28
Macarena	25
Pipa Club	10
Sidecar	11
So-da	18
Tarantos	15
Travel Bar	7

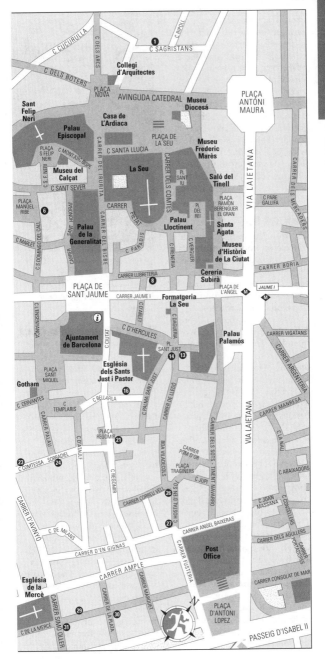

(daily 10.30am–6pm; €2) – the elevator (*ascensor als terrats*) is just to the left of the crypt steps – which provides intimate views of the cathedral towers and surrounding Gothic buildings.

Performances of the Catalan national dance, the *sardana*, take place in front of the cathedral (Feb–July & Sept–Nov Sat 6.30pm & Sun noon), while the wide, pedestrianized Avinguda de la Catedral also hosts an antiques market every Thursday, and a Christmas craft fair every December.

Plaça del Rei

The most concentrated batch of historic monuments in the Barri Gòtic is the grouping around the neat Plaça del Rei. The square was once the courtyard of the palace of the counts of Barcelona, and across it stairs climb to the fourteenth-century **Saló del Tinell**, the palace's main hall. It was on the steps leading from the Saló del Tinell into the Plaça del Rei that Ferdinand and Isabella stood to receive Columbus on his triumphant return from his famous voyage of 1492. At one time the Spanish Inquisition met here, taking full advantage of the popular belief that the walls would move if a lie was spoken. Nowadays it hosts temporary exhibitions, while concerts are occasionally held in the hall or outside in the square. The palace buildings also include the fourteenth-century **Capella de Santa Agata**, with its tall single nave and fine Gothic retable, and the Renaissance **Torre del Rei Martí**, which rises above one corner of the square. There's currently no public access to the tower, but the interiors of the hall and chapel can be seen

▲ ARTISTS' MARKET, PLAÇA SANT JOSEP ORIEL

during a visit to the Museu d'Història de la Ciutat (see below).

Museu d'Història de la Ciutat

Pl. del Rei, entrance on c/del Veguer ☎933 151 111, ⊛www.museuhistoria .bcn.es. June–Sept Tues–Sat 10am–8pm, Sun 10am–3pm; Oct–May Tues–Sat 10am–2pm & 4–8pm, Sun 10am–3pm. €4, first Sat afternoon of the month free. The crucial draw of the City History Museum is its underground archeological section – nothing less than the extensive remains of the Roman city of Barcino. Descending in the elevator (the floor indicator shows "12 BC"), you are deposited onto walkways that run along the 4000 square metres excavated thus far, stretching under Plaça del Rei and the surrounding streets as far as the cathedral. The remains date from the first century BC to the sixth century AD and, while not much survives above chest height, explanatory diagrams show the extent of the streets, walls and buildings –

from lookout towers to laundries – while models, mosaics, murals and excavated goods help flesh out the reality of daily life in Barcino.

The museum also offers visitors the chance to see the interiors of the Plaça del Rei's finest buildings, and learn something of the city's long history. For a bit more depth, ask about the museum walking tours of the Plaça del Rei ensemble (2hr; €5–7, in English by arrangement).

Museu Frederic Marès

Pl. de Sant Iu 5–6 ☎933 105 800, ⓦwww.museumares.bcn.es. Tues–Sat 10am–7pm, Sun 10am–3pm. €3, Wed afternoon & first Sun of month free.
Frederic Marès (1893–1991) was a sculptor, painter and restorer who more or less single-handedly restored Catalunya's decaying medieval treasures in the early twentieth century. The ground and basement floors of the museum consist of his personal collection of medieval sculpture – an important body of work that includes a comprehensive collection of wooden crucifixes showing the stylistic development of this form from the twelfth to the fifteenth centuries. However, it's the upper two floors, housing Marès' personal collectibles, which tend to make jaws drop. Entire rooms are devoted to keys and locks, pipes, cigarette cards and snuffboxes, fans, gloves and brooches, playing cards, draughtsmen's tools, walking sticks, dolls' houses, toy theatres, old gramophones and archaic bicycles, to list just a sample of what's on show. The large arcaded museum courtyard, studded with orange trees, is one of the most romantic in the

old town, and the summer café here (*Café d'Estiu*; open April–Oct, closed Mon) makes a perfect place to take a break from sightseeing.

Església de Santa María del Pi

Pl. Sant Josep Oriol ☎933 184 743, ⓦwww.parroquiadelpi.com. The fourteenth-century church of Santa María is mainly Catalan-Gothic in style though with a Romanesque door. The rather plain interior only serves to set off some marvellous stained glass, the most impressive of which is contained within a ten-metre-wide rose window. The church flanks Plaça Sant Josep Oriol, the prettiest of three adjacent squares, an ideal place to take an outdoor coffee, listen to the buskers and browse the weekend **artists' market** (Sat 11am–8pm, Sun 11am–2pm).

The church is named – like the squares on either side, Plaça del Pi and Placeta del Pi – after the pine tree that once stood here. A **farmers' market** spills across Plaça del Pi on the first and third Friday and Saturday of the month, selling honey, cheese, cakes and other produce, while **Carrer de Petritxol** (off Plaça del Pi) is the place to come for a hot chocolate in one of the traditional cafés that still thrive here.

Sala Parés

C/de Petritxol 5–8 ☎933 187 020, ⓦwww.salapares.com. Mon–Sat 10.30am–2pm & 5–8.30pm; closed Aug. Possibly the most famous commercial art gallery in the city, established in the mid-nineteenth century, Sala Parés is well-known as the site of

▲ SALA PARÉS

Picasso's first solo exhibition. It still deals exclusively in nineteenth- and twentieth-century Catalan art and you're free to browse the regularly changing exhibitions.

Museu del Calçat

Pl. Sant Felip Neri 5 ☎ 933 014 533. Tues–Sun 11am–2pm. €2.50. The former headquarters of the city's shoemakers' guild (founded in 1202) houses a one-room footwear museum, containing originals dating back to the 1600s as well as oddities like the world's biggest shoe, made for the city's Columbus statue. The museum flanks one side of Plaça Sant Felip Neri, whose eponymous church still bears the marks of bomb damage sustained during the Civil War. Incidentally, Barcelona's medieval Jewish quarter lay just to the south of Plaça Sant Felip Neri, centred on today's c/Sant Domènec del Call (*Call* is the Catalan word for a narrow passage). A plaque at c/Sant Domènec del Call 7 marks the site of the synagogue, while the Jewish baths are believed to have been located somewhere on c/de Banys Nous.

Plaça de Sant Jaume

The spacious square at the end of the main c/de Ferran was once the site of Barcelona's Roman forum and marketplace. It's now the traditional site of demonstrations and gatherings, as well as being one venue for the weekly dancing of the Catalan folk dance, the **sardana** (Sunday at 6.30pm). Participants all hold hands in a circle, each puts something in the middle as a sign of community and sharing, and, since it is not over-energetic (hence the jibes of other Spaniards) old and young can join in equally. The accompanying instrumental group is called a *cobla*, and it includes the *flabiol* (a type of long flute), the *tambori* (drum), and tenor and soprano oboes.

Ajuntament de Barcelona

Pl. de Sant Jaume ☎ 934 027 000. Public admitted Sun 10am–2pm. Free. On the south side of Plaça de Sant Jaume stands Barcelona's city hall, parts of which date from as early as 1373. On Sundays you're allowed into the building to see the most interesting part, the restored fourteenth-century council chamber, the Saló de Cent, on the first floor. To view the former main entrance, head a little way down c/de la Ciutat to find a typically exuberant Catalan-Gothic facade that was badly damaged during renovations in the nineteenth century.

Palau de la Generalitat

Pl. de Sant Jaume ☎ 934 024 600. Tours on 2nd and 4th Sun of the month (not Aug), every 20min, 10am–2pm;

also on April 23, and Sept 11 & 24. Free. The traditional home of the Catalan government presents its best – or at least its oldest – aspect around the side on c/del Bisbe, where the early fifteenth-century facade contains a medallion portraying St George and the dragon. (Incidentally, the enclosed Gothic bridge across the narrow street – the so-called Bridge of Sighs – is an anachronism, added in 1928.) Through the palace's Renaissance main entrance, facing Plaça de Sant Jaume, there's a beautiful cloister on the first floor with superb coffered ceilings, while opening off this gallery are two fine rooms – the chapel and salon of Sant Jordi (St George, patron saint of Catalunya as well as England). You can visit the interior on a guided tour on alternate Sundays while the Generalitat is also traditionally open on public holidays, particularly April 23 – the **Dia de Sant Jordi** (St George's Day). Celebrated as a nationalist holiday in Catalunya, this is also a kind of local Valentine's Day, when men give their sweethearts a rose and receive a book in return (although, in recent years, modernization has demanded books for women and roses for men as well). The Generalitat's precincts are packed with book stalls and rose sellers on this day, with huge queues forming to get in the building.

Església dels Sants Just i Pastor

Pl. de Sant Just 6 ☎ 933 017 433. Open for Mass at 7.30pm (Sun at noon) and occasional other times. Plaça de Sant Just is a medieval gem, sporting a restored fourteenth-century fountain and flanked by unassuming palaces. Highlight here is the Església dels Sants Just i Pastor, whose very plain stone facade belies the rich stained glass and elaborate chapel decoration inside (enter from the back, at c/de la Ciutat; the main doors on Pl. de Sant Just are open less often). The name commemorates the city's earliest Christian martyrs, and it's claimed (though there's no real evidence) that this is the oldest

▼ IRON LAMPS, PLAÇA REIAL

▲ PLAÇA GEORGE ORWELL

parish church site in Barcelona, held to have first supported a foundation at the beginning of the ninth century.

Plaça Reial

The elegant nineteenth-century Plaça Reial is hidden behind an archway off the Ramblas. Laid out in around 1850, the Italianate square is studded with tall palm trees and decorated iron lamps (designed by the young Antoni Gaudí), bordered by high, pastel-coloured arcaded buildings, and centred on a fountain depicting the Three Graces. Taking in the sun at one of the benches or pavement cafés puts you in mixed company – punks, bikers, buskers, Catalan eccentrics, tramps and bemused tourists. It used to be a bit dodgy in Plaça Reial, but most of the really unsavoury characters have been driven off over the years as tourists have staked an increasing claim to the square. Nonetheless, keep an eye on your belongings, and don't expect to see too many locals until night falls, when the surrounding bars come into

their own. If you pass through on a Sunday morning, look in on the **coin and stamp market** (10am–2pm).

Carrer d'Avinyo

Carrer d'Avinyo, running south from c/de Ferran towards the harbour, cuts through the most atmospheric part of the southern Barri Gòtic. It used to be a red-light district of some renown, and was frequented by the young Picasso, whose family moved into the area in 1895. It still looks the part – a narrow thoroughfare lined with dark overhanging buildings – but the fashionable cafés and boutiques tell the story of its creeping gentrification. A few rough edges still show, particularly around **Plaça George Orwell**, whose low steps and funky bars are a favoured hangout for the grunge crowd.

Carrer de la Mercè

In the eighteenth century, the neighbourhood known as La Mercè – just a block from the harbour – was an aristocratic address, home to the many nobles and merchants enriched by Barcelona's maritime trade. Most fashionable families took the opportunity to move north to the Eixample later in the nineteenth century, and the streets of La Mercè took on an earthier hue. Since then, Carrer de la Mercè and surrounding streets have been home to a series of characteristic old-style taverns known as *tascas* or *bodegas* – a glass of wine from the barrel in *Bodega la Plata* (see p.69), or a similar joint, is one of the old town's more authentic experiences.

At Plaça de la Mercè, the eighteenth-century **Església de la Mercè** is the focus of the city's biggest annual celebration, the Festa de la Mercè (see p.191) every September, dedicated to the patroness of Barcelona. The square outside was remodelled in the twentieth century around its statue of Neptune.

Shops

L'Arca del Avia

C/Banys Nous 20 ☏ 933 021 598. Catalan brides used to fill up their nuptial trunk (*l'arca*) with embroidered bed linen and lace. Period (eighteenth-, nineteenth- and early twentieth-century) costumes can be hired or purchased as well – Kate Winslet's *Titanic* costume came from here.

Art Escudellers

C/Escudellers 23–25 ☏ 934 126 801, ⊛ www.escudellers-art.com. Enormous shop selling a wide range of ceramics, glass, jewellery and decorated tiles from different regions of Spain. Shipping can be arranged, and there's also a gourmet wine and food section.

Cerería Subirà

Bxda. Llibreteria 7 ☏ 933 152 606. Barcelona's oldest shop (since 1760) has a beautiful interior, selling unique handcrafted candles.

Formatgeria La Seu

C/Dagueria 16 ☏ 934 126 548. Closed Mon. The best farmhouse cheeses from independent producers all over Spain. Catherine, who's Scottish, will introduce you into the world of cheese with Saturday cheese tastings (noon–3pm; €5).

Futura

C/Escudellers 56 ☏ 933 174 975. Argentinean designer producing clothes from interesting, colourful fabrics.

Gotham

C/Cervantes 7 ☏ 934 124 647. The place to come for retro furniture, lighting and accessories from all periods from the 1930s to 1970s, plus original designs.

▼ PLAÇA DUC DE MEDINACELI

Herboristeria del Rey

C/del Vidre 1 ☎ 933 180 512. An early nineteenth-century herbalist's shop, tucked off Plaça Reial, which stocks more than 250 medicinal herbs designed to combat all complaints.

Llibreria Quera

C/Petritxol 2 ☎ 933 180 743, ⓦ www.llibreriaquera.com. Closed Sat in Aug. Best and most knowledgeable place in town for Catalan maps and trekking guides, though it's a bit of a squeeze in the cramped little store.

▲ ESPADRILLES, MANUAL ALPARGATERA

Manual Alpargatera

C/d'Avinyó 7 ☎ 933 010 172, ⓦ www.lamanualalpargatera.com. This traditional workshop makes and sells *alpargatas* (espadrilles) to order, as well as producing other straw and rope work.

El Mercadillo

C/Portaferrissa 17 ☎ 933 018 913. Double-decker complex of shops selling skate-, club- and beachwear and shoes – look out for the camel marking the entrance. There's a bar upstairs with a nice patio garden.

Cafés

Bar del Pi

Pl. Sant Josep Oriol 1 ☎ 933 022 123. Mon–Sat 9am–11pm, Sun 10am–10pm; closed 2 weeks in Jan & Aug. Small café-bar best known for its terrace on one of Barcelona's prettiest squares. Service can be slow – not that anyone's in a hurry in this prime people-watching spot.

Cereria

Bxda. de Sant Miquel 3–5 ☎ 933 058 110. Mon–Sat 10am–10pm. Amiably hip café where the decor is thrift-store chic, with piles of old papers and magazines to while away the hours. Food is breakfast- and veggie-friendly, with great-looking cakes and a changing roster of daily specials.

Mesón del Cafe

C/Llibreteria 16 ☎ 933 150 754. Mon–Sat 7am–11pm. Offbeat locals' bar where you'll probably have to stand to sample the pastries and the excellent coffee – including a cappuccino laden with fresh cream.

Venus Delicatessen

C/d'Avinyó 25 ☎ 933 011 585. Mon–Sat noon–midnight. Med-bistro cuisine available throughout the day and night. It's good for vegetarians, with lasagne, couscous, moussaka and salads all costing around €5–9, and there's a well-priced weekday lunchtime *menú del dia* too.

Xaloc

C/Palla 13–17 ☎ 933 011 990. Mon–Thurs & Sun 9am–midnight, Fri & Sat 9am–1am. A contemporary *xarcuteria* and deli – so you can get any kind of cured meat and cheese in your sandwich – but it's also an airy place to stop for

▲ COURTYARD CAFÉ, EL MERCADILLO SHOPPING CENTRE

a coffee. The *menú del dia* is €10.

Restaurants and tapas bars

Bar Celta Pulpería

C/de la Mercè 16 ☎933 150 006. Mon–Sat 10am–1am. This no-nonsense brightly lit Galician tapas bar specializes in octopus, fried *pimientos* (peppers) and heady regional wine. It's best to ask prices as you go here – the food's good but the bill has a habit of mounting up, especially for out-of-towners.

Bodega la Plata

C/de la Mercè 28 ☎933 151 009. Daily 10am–4pm & 8–11pm. A classic taste of the old town, with a marble counter open to the street and wine straight from the barrel. Anchovies are the speciality (salted and laid over cut tomatoes or deep-fried, like whitebait), attracting an enthusiastic local crowd, from pre-clubbers to businessmen.

Café de l'Acadèmia

C/Lledó 1 ☎933 198 253. Mon–Fri 9am–noon, 1.30–4pm & 8.45–11.30pm; closed 2 weeks in Aug. Creative Catalan cooking in a romantic stone-flagged restaurant with lovely summer *terrassa*. Dishes range from confit of *bacallà* (salt cod) with spinach and pine kernels to aubergine terrine with goat's cheese, plus grills, fresh fish and rice. Prices are very reasonable (mains €10–16) and it's always busy, so dinner reservations are essential. A no-choice *menú del dia* (€11.50, €8 at the bar) is a bargain for the quality; a nice breakfast is served too.

Ginger

C/Palma Sant Just 1 ☎933 105 309. Tues–Sat 7pm–3am; closed 2 weeks in Aug. Cocktails and creative tapas in a groovy 1970s-style setting. It's a world away from *patatas bravas* and battered squid – think roast duck vinaigrette, tuna tartare and vegetarian satay for around €5–7 a pop.

Irati

C/Cardenal Casañas 17 ☎933 023 084. Tues–Sun noon–midnight; *pintxos* served noon–3pm & 7–11pm. Crowded brick-walled bar where locals think favourably of the *pintxos* (Basque tapas, pinned with sticks to a baguette slice), which run the gamut from country sausage to smoked salmon. There's a seasonally changing Basque menu in the restaurant if finger food isn't your thing, with mains around €18–20.

Juicy Jones

C/Cardenal Casañas 7 ☎933 024 330. Daily 10am–midnight. Veggie-vegan restaurant/juice bar with a €9 *menú del dia* that touches all corners of the world – say

▲ CARRER DE LA PALLA

cashew, carrot and coriander soup followed by pumpkin-stuffed gnocchi. The restaurant is in a mural-and-graffiti-ridden cellar at the back – juices are squeezed and soy milkshakes whizzed at the front bar.

Limbo

C/de la Mercè 13 ☎933 107 699. Mon–Thurs & Sun 9pm–midnight, Fri & Sat 9pm–1am; closed 2 weeks in Aug. Designer restaurant with an intimate feel, presenting an interesting fusion of modern and traditional Catalan cuisine, like tuna with goat's cheese or perch served in a Thai-style curry. Most main dishes cost €11–16.

Matsuri

Pl. Regomir 1 ☎932 681 535. Mon–Fri 1.30–3.30pm & 8–11.30pm, Sat 8–11.30pm. Excellent Southeast Asian cuisine, concentrating on noodles, Thai salads and curries. Service is friendly, and the wooden Indonesian-style furniture and terracotta colours make for a relaxed meal. Around €25 a head.

Oolong

C/d'en Gignas 25 ☎933 151 259. Daily 8pm–1am. Refined fusion food in an informal setting, with dinner costing up to €30. The short menu changes weekly, but Asian, Mediterranean and South American flavours set the tone – dishes like asparagus tempura and stuffed pork loin grab diners' taste buds. It's only small, so reservations are advised.

Salón

C/l'Hostal d'en Sol 6–8 ☎933 152 159. Mon–Sat 1.30–4.30pm & 8.30pm–midnight; closed 2 weeks in Aug. Old building with a Gothic sort of feel, serving imaginative dishes in a relaxed bistro atmosphere. The menu ranges far and wide from, say, rabbit with a *mole* sauce and tacos to curried vegetables with a yoghurt and coconut sauce. Mains cost €12–15, or there's a weekday lunchtime *menú del dia* at €9.50; you can stay late and drink at the bar too.

Shunka

C/Sagristans 5 ☎934 124 991. Tues–Fri 1.30–3.30pm & 8.30–11.30pm, Sat & Sun 2–4pm & 8.30–11.30pm; closed 2 weeks in Aug. The locals think this is the best Japanese restaurant in the old town – it's certainly always busy, so make an advance reservation, sit back and enjoy. You can have the works for

€30, though sushi and a drink at the bar by the open kitchen is an enjoyable compromise.

Veronica

C/d'Avinyo 30 ☎ 934 121 122. Daily noon–1am; closed 2 weeks in Aug. Crispy pizzas (all bar one vegetarian) and inventive salads are served at tables on funky Plaça George Orwell, which catches the sun during the day. At night there's a bit of a gay scene as the urban-chic bar-restaurant comes into play.

Vinissim

C/Sant Domènec del Call 12 ☎ 933 014 575. Tues–Sun noon–4pm & 6pm–1am. Upscale tavern food – sliced meats, salads, *torrades* (toasted bread with tomato and oil) – accompanied by fine Catalan wines available by the glass. Lunch (€13) outside on Plaça Manuel Ribe is a treat on a warm day.

Bars

Ascensor

C/Bellafila 3 ☎ 933 185 347. Daily 6pm–3am. Old lift doors and control panel signal the entrance to this popular local bar. It's not at all touristy, and has a comfortable feel – great for a late-night drink and a natter.

Café Royale

C/Nou de Zurbano 3 ☎ 934 121 433. Daily 7pm–3am. Sleek lounge bar where all the beautiful people get together to show off their best moves to the Latin jazz, soul and funky tunes. A conundrum: arrive after midnight and you'll have to join the queue; come too early and you'll be on your own.

Glaciar

Pl. Reial 3 ☎ 933 021 163. Mon–Thurs 4pm–2am, Fri & Sat 4pm–3am, Sun 9am–2am. At this traditional Barcelona meeting point the terrace seating is packed out most sunny evenings and at weekends.

Leticia

C/de Codols 21 ☎ 933 020 074. Daily except Tues 7pm–3am. Cosy bar with mellow sounds and a laid-back clientele – the sofa at the back is the seat in demand. Monthly art exhibitions add some colour, while sandwiches, salads and cakes are served until late.

Pipa Club

Pl. Reial 3 ☎ 933 024 732, ⊕ www.bpipaclub.com. Daily 11pm–3am. Historically a pipe-smoker's haunt, it's a wood-panelled, jazzy, late-night kind of place – ring the bell for

▼ PICASSO FRIEZE ON COLLEGI D'ARQUITECTES

admission and make your way up the stairs.

So-da

C/d'Avinyó 24 ☏ 934 122 776. Daily 9pm–2.30am. In the daytime this place is a cutting-edge urban clothes store; at night the designer rags are locked away into cupboards and the place turns into a wicked bar, with comfy armchairs and tasty cocktails.

Travel Bar

C/Boqueria 27 ☏ 933 425 252, ⊛ www.travelbar.com. Mon–Thurs & Sun 9am–2am, Fri & Sat 9am–3am. Backpacking Catalans have brought their experiences home to provide a bar where travellers can hang out and meet like-minded souls, sign up for tours, check their email and generally chill out.

Clubs

Fonfone

C/dels Escudellers 24 ☏ 933 171 424, ⊛ www.fonfone.com. Daily 10pm–3am. Attracts a young crowd into fast, hard music, though it changes mood sometimes with satin soul and best-of-1980s nights.

Harlem Jazz Club

C/Comtessa de Sobradiel 8 ☏ 933 100 755. Closed Aug. Small, usually jam-packed venue for mixed jazz styles, from African and Gypsy to flamenco and fusion; live music nightly at 10.30pm and midnight (weekends 11.30pm & 1am). Cover charge up to €5.

Jamboree

Pl. Reial 17 ☏ 933 191 789, ⊛ www.masimas.com. Jazz gigs nightly at 11pm and 12.30am, and then you stay on for the club, playing funk, swing, hip-hop and R&B. Admission €6–10.

Karma

Pl. Reial 10 ☏ 933 025 680. Tues–Sun 11.30pm–5am. A studenty basement place that can get claustrophobic at times. Sounds are indie, Britpop and US college, while a lively local crowd mills around the square outside.

Macarena

C/Nou de Sant Francesc 5; no phone. Mon–Thurs & Sun 11pm–4am, Fri & Sat 11pm–5am. Once a place where flamenco tunes were offered up to La Macarena, the Virgin of Seville. Now it's a heaving, funky, electronic temple with a tolerant crowd – they have to be, as there's not much space. Entry usually free.

Sidecar

C/Heures 4–6, Pl. Reial ☏ 933 021 586. Tues–Sun 11pm–4.30am. Hip music club – pronounced "See-day-car" – with nightly gigs and DJs that champion rock, pop, fusion and urban styles. Class local acts like GoLem System appear regularly; entry from €6.

Tarantos

Pl. Reial 17 ☏ 933 191 789, ⊛ www.masimas.com. Barcelona's oldest flamenco show has nightly performances at 10pm, plus other jazz, funk and tango gigs (entry from around €10), followed by Latin and world music sounds until 5am with the resident DJ.

Port Vell and Barceloneta

Barcelona has an urban waterfront that merges seamlessly with the old town, providing an easy escape from the claustrophobic medieval streets. The harbour at the bottom of the Ramblas has been thoroughly overhauled in recent years and Port Vell (Old Port), as it's now known, presents a series of heavyweight tourist attractions, from sightseeing boats to a maritime museum – not to mention the shops, bars and restaurants of the entertainment centre called Maremàgnum. By way of contrast, Barceloneta – the wedge of land to the east, backing the marina – retains its eighteenth-century character, and the former fishing quarter is still the most popular place to come and eat paella, fish and seafood. Metro Drassanes, at the bottom of the Ramblas, is the best starting point for Port Vell; Barceloneta has its own metro station.

Mirador de Colón

Pl. Portal de la Pau ☎933 025 224. April & May daily 10am-7.30pm; June–Sept daily 9am–8.30pm; Oct–March Mon–Fri 10am–1.30pm & 3.30–6.30pm, Sat & Sun 10am–6.30pm. €2. The striking monument at the foot of the Ramblas commemorates the visit made by Christopher Columbus to Barcelona in June 1493, when the Italian-born navigator was received in style by the Catholic monarchs Ferdinand and Isabella. Columbus tops a grandiose iron column, 52m high, guarded by lions, around which unfold reliefs telling the story of his life and travels – here, if nowhere else, the old mercenary is still the "discoverer of America". You can ride the lift up to the enclosed viewing platform at Columbus's feet, from where the 360-degree views are terrific. Meanwhile, from the quayside in front of the Columbus monument, Las Golondrinas sightseeing boats depart on regular trips throughout the year around the inner harbour – see p.190.

see p.190.

▼ MIRADOR DE COLÓN

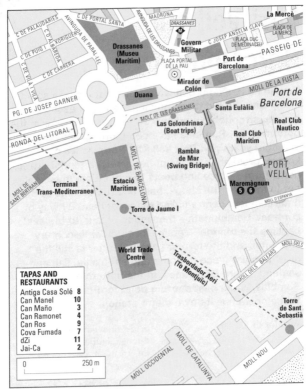

TAPAS AND RESTAURANTS

Antiga Casa Solé	8
Can Manel	10
Can Maño	3
Can Ramonet	4
Can Ros	9
Cova Fumada	7
dZi	11
Jai-Ca	2

Museu Marítim

Avgda. de les Drassanes ☎ 933 429 920, ⓦ www.diba.es/mmaritim. Daily 10am–7pm. €5.40. Barcelona's unique medieval shipyards, or Drassanes, date from the thirteenth century and were in continuous use – fitting and arming Catalunya's war fleet or trading vessels – until well into the eighteenth century. Today, the huge, stone-vaulted buildings make a fitting home for the enjoyable Maritime Museum, whose centrepiece is a full-scale copy of a sixteenth-century royal galley which was originally constructed here. This is surrounded by different thematic sections covering Catalunya's relationship with the sea and containing sailing boats, figureheads, old maps and charts, navigation instruments and other nautical bits and pieces. There's a good restaurant at the museum, while the café puts out tables in the pleasant courtyard.

Santa Eulàlia

Moll de la Fusta; no phone. Tues–Fri noon–5.30pm, Sat & Sun 10am–5.30pm. €2.40, free with Museu Marítim ticket. The three-masted ocean-going schooner *Santa Eulàlia* is a flagship showpiece of the nearby Museu Marítim. Dating from 1908, as the *Carmen*

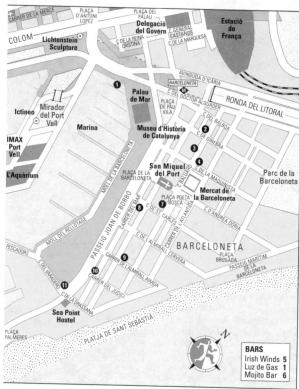

Flores it once made the run between Barcelona and Cuba, but was subsequently acquired by the museum and fully restored. A short tour lets you walk the deck and shows off the interior.

Maremàgnum

Moll d'Espanya ☏ 932 258 100, ⓦwww.maremagnum.es. Daily 11am–11pm. From near the Columbus statue, the wooden Rambla de Mar swing bridge strides across the harbour to Maremàgnum on Moll d'Espanya, a typically bold piece of Catalan design, the soaring glass lines of the leisure complex tempered by the surrounding undulating wooden walkways. Inside are two floors of gift shops and boutiques (including an official FC Barcelona merchandise store), plus a wide range of bars and restaurants with harbourside seating and high prices. It's a fun place to come at night, though no self-respecting local would rate the food as anything but ordinary. Outside, benches and park areas provide scintillating views back across the harbour to the city.

L'Aquàrium

Moll d'Espanya ☏ 932 217 474, ⓦwww.aquariumbcn.com. Daily: July & Aug 9.30am–11pm; Sept–June

▲ PORT DE BARCELONA BUILDING

9.30am–9pm, until 9.30pm at weekends. €13.50. Adjacent to Maremàgnum, Port Vell's high-profile aquarium drags in families and school parties throughout the year to see "a magical world, full of mystery". Or, to be more precise, to see fish and sea creatures in 21 themed tanks representing underwater caves, tidal areas, tropical reefs, the planet's oceans and other maritime habitats. It's vastly overpriced, and despite the claims of excellence it offers few new experiences, save perhaps the eighty-metre-long walk-through underwater tunnel which brings you face to face with gliding rays and cruising sharks. Some child-centred displays and activities, and a nod towards ecology and conservation matters, pad out the attractions, before you're tipped out in the aquarium shop so they can part you from even more of your money.

IMAX Port Vell

Moll d'Espanya ☎932 251 111, ⊕www.imaxportvell.com. Screenings 11am–10.30pm, later at weekends. Tickets €7 or €10. Barcelona's IMAX theatre stands next to the aquarium, with three screens showing films virtually hourly in 3D or in giant format. The themes are familiar – the mysteries of the human body,

alien adventure, etc – but you'll find that the films are in Spanish or Catalan only. If this puts you off, saunter down instead to the sloping lawn nearby to examine the replica of the strange fish-shaped submarine, the **Ictineo**, a genuine Catalan curiosity, invented in the mid-nineteenth century by radical visionary Narcís Monturiol i Estarriol.

▲ MARISCAL CRAYFISH, PORT VELL

Museu d'Història de Catalunya

Palau de Mar, Pl. de Pau Vila 3 ☎932 254 700, ⊕www.mhcat.net. Tues & Thurs–Sat 10am–7pm, Wed 10am–8pm, Sun 10am–2.30pm. €3, first Sun of month and public holidays free. The only surviving warehouse on the Port Vell harbourside is known as the Palau de Mar, home to an enterprising museum tracing the history of Catalunya from the

Stone Age to the twentieth century. There are temporary shows on the ground floor, while a lift takes you up to the permanent displays: second floor for year dot to the Industrial Revolution, and third for periods and events up to 1980 (though later coverage is planned). You can pick up full English notes at the desk, and there's plenty to get your teeth into, whether it's poking around the interior of a Roman grain ship or comparing the rival nineteenth-century architectural plans for the Eixample. On the fourth floor, the café-bar boasts a glorious view from its huge terrace of the harbour, Tibidabo, Montjuïc and the city skyline – you don't need a museum ticket to visit this.

The seafood restaurants in the **Palau de Mar** arcade below the museum are some of the most popular in the city, especially at weekends. Here you overlook the packed **marina**, where Catalans park their yachts like they park their cars – impossibly tightly – fronted in summer by hawkers spreading blankets on the ground to sell jewellery and sunglasses.

Barceloneta

There's no finer place for lunch on a sunny day than the Barceloneta neighbourhood, bound by the harbour on one side and the Mediterranean on the other. Laid out in 1755 as a classic eighteenth-century grid, its long, narrow streets are still very much as they were planned, broken at intervals by small squares – like Plaça de la Barceloneta, with its eighteenth-century fountain and Neoclassical church of **Sant Miquel del Port**. The adjacent

Plaça de la Font holds the local market, **Mercat de la Barceloneta** (Mon–Sat 7am–3pm, plus Fri 4.30–8.30pm except in Aug), while the seafood restaurants that are the neighbourhood's *raison d'être* are found scattered right across the tight grid of streets but most characteristically lined along the harbourside Passeig Joan de Borbó.

Passeig Marítim

A double row of palms backs the sweeping stone esplanade that runs from Barceloneta's beach, Platja de Sant Sebastià, as far as the Port Olímpic. It's a fifteen-minute walk from Barceloneta to the port, but some do it much quicker than that – the Passeig Marítim is a notable track for bladers, skaters and joggers, who have one of the Med's best views for company.

▼ PLAÇA DE LA BARCELONETA

▲ ICTINEO, PORT VELL

On the way, just before the hospital and port, you'll pass the **Parc de la Barceloneta**, a rather plain expanse enlivened only by its whimsical *modernista* water tower (1905), rising like a minaret above the palms.

Trasbordador Aeri

Torre de Sant Sebastiá, Barceloneta ☎933 321 164. Daily 10.45am–7pm. €7.50 one-way, €9 return. The most thrilling ride in the city centre is across the inner harbour on the cable car, which sweeps over the water from the foot of Barceloneta to Montjuïc. The views are stunning, and you can pick out with ease the familiar towers of La Seu and Sagrada Família, while the trees

▼ MENÚ DEL DIA SIGN, BARCELONETA

lining the Ramblas look like the forked tongue of a serpent. Departures are every fifteen minutes, though in summer and at weekends you may have to wait for a while at the top of the towers for a ride as the cars only carry about twenty people at a time.

Restaurants and tapas bars

Antiga Casa Solé

C/Sant Carles 4 ☎932 215 012. Tues–Sat 1–4pm & 8–11pm, Sun 1–4pm. Founded in 1903, it was here that *sarsuela* (Catalan fish stew) was invented. Since then, the quiet, formal restaurant has been dishing up market-fresh fish and seafood, either in stews or casseroles (*suquets*) or simply grilled, sautéed or mixed with rice. Count on a good €40 a head – and reserve ahead for dinner.

Can Manel

Pg. Joan de Borbó 60 ☎932 215 013. Daily 1–4pm & 8pm–midnight. An institution since 1870, which fills very quickly, inside and out, because the food is both good and reasonably priced. Paella, *fideuà* (noodles with seafood) and *arròs a banda* (rice with seafood) are staples, while grilled fish always costs more. A weekday lunchtime *menú del dia* keeps the cost down, but there's usually not much fish or seafood choice on this.

Can Maño

C/Baluard 12 ☏ 933 193 082. Mon–Fri 8am–5.30pm & 8.30–11pm, Sat 8am–5pm; closed Aug. There's rarely a tourist in sight in this old-fashioned locals' diner. Fried or grilled fish is the thing here (sardines, mullet, calamari), though there are some daily specials and basic meat dishes, rough house wine and absolutely no frills. It's an authentic experience, which is likely to cost you less than €10 a head.

Can Ramonet

C/Maquinista 17 ☏ 933 193 064. Daily 10am–4pm & 8pm–midnight; closed Sun dinner & Aug. Reputedly the oldest restaurant in the port area, it has the added attraction of a shady *terrassa*. Seafood meals can turn out pricey (mains €15–20) but you can always hunker down instead in the rustic front bar, where the tapas is piled high on wooden barrels – the *pernil* (cured ham) is a house speciality.

Can Ros

C/Almirall Aixada 7 ☏ 932 215 049. Daily 1–5pm & 8pm–midnight; closed Wed. This is one of the best places to sample paella, *arròs negre* ("black rice", ie made with cuttlefish ink) or a *fideuà* (noodles) with clams and shrimp, all of which cost around €10. The tables are packed in close together, but it's a comfortable, no-hurry kind of place.

Cova Fumada

C/Baluard 56 ☏ 932 214 061. Mon–Fri 9am–3pm & 6–8pm, Sat 9am–3pm.

Come for a gregarious lunch in this busy traditional tapas bar. The seafood is straight from the market, and if you want the house speciality ask for the *bombas* (spicy meatballs).

dZi

Pg. Joan de Borbó 76 ☏ 932 212 182. Daily 1–4pm & 8pm–midnight. It's pronounced "zhee", which is a Tibetan sacred stone, but the lovely fresh-tasting food is Southeast Asian, mainly Chinese, Malaysian and Japanese, either served in the serene dining room or outside on the shady *terrassa*. Yu-shian pork with aubergine or Formosa-style shrimps with ginger are great bets, with green-tea ice cream amongst the desserts. About €25 a head, though you can eat for €10 or so at lunch.

▼ ROY LICHTENSTEIN SCULPTURE

▲ BOARDWALK, PLATJA DE SANT SEBASTIÀ

Jai-Ca

C/Ginebra 13 ☎932 683 265. Daily
10am–11pm. Scrutinize the tapas
list on the wall or just check
what your neighbour's having –
a bundle of *navajas* (razor
clams), say, or some plump
anchovies. Meanwhile, the fryers
in the kitchen work overtime,
turning out crisp baby squid
and little green peppers
scattered with salt. Take your
haul to a tile-topped cane table,
or outside onto the
tiny street-corner
patio.

Bars

Irish Winds

Maremàgnum ☎932 258
187. Mon–Thurs & Sun
12.30pm–4am, Fri & Sat
12.30pm–5am. A pretty
good place to catch
Irish/Celtic folk, with
live music in the pub
around 11pm most
nights.

Luz de Gas

Moll del Diposit, in front of
Palau de Mar ☎932 097
711, ⊛www.luzdegas.com.
March–Oct daily noon–3am.
Sip a chilled drink on
the polished deck of
the moored boat, and
soak up some great
marina and harbour
views. Queues form
on hot days, when
every parasol-shaded
seat is taken, but it's
especially nice at dusk
as the city lights begin
to twinkle.

Mojito Bar

Maremàgnum ☎933 528 746. Daily
5pm–5am. Themed Caribbean
playhouse, with tropical decor,
cocktails and free daily salsa
classes. The *salsoteca* packs them
in on Friday and Saturday
nights, and there's live music
with the Cuban big band on
Sunday.

El Raval

The old-town neighbourhood of El Raval, on the west side of the Ramblas, was traditionally known as a red-light area. It still has some very seedy corners (particularly south of Carrer de Sant Pau), though it's changing rapidly, notably in the "upper Raval" around Barcelona's contemporary art museum, MACBA, from which ripple out cutting-edge galleries, see-and-be-seen restaurants and fashionable bars. Historically, El Raval (from the Arabic word for suburb) stood outside the medieval city walls, housing hospitals, churches and monasteries, and noxious trades like slaughterhouses (tallers, hence the street name Carrer dels Tallers) that had no place in the more refined Gothic quarter. Throughout most of the twentieth century, the neighbourhood was notorious for its sleazy Barri Xinès (China Town), though regeneration has cleaned up large parts of El Raval, and now a younger, artier, more affluent population rubs shoulders with the area's Asian and North African immigrants and the older, traditional residents. Metros Catalunya, Liceu, Drassanes and Paral.lel serve the neighbourhood.

Museu d'Art Contemporani de Barcelona (MACBA)

Pl. dels Àngels 1 ☏934 120 810, ⓦwww.macba.es. June–Sept Mon & Wed–Fri 11am–8pm, Sat 10am–8pm, Sun 10am–3pm; rest of the year closes weekdays 7.30pm. €7, Wed €3, special exhibitions €4. Anchoring the northern reaches of the Raval is the Museu d'Art Contemporani de Barcelona (MACBA), whose main facade is entirely constructed of glass. Once inside, you go from the ground to the fourth floor up a series of swooping ramps, which afford continuous views of the square below – usually full of careering skateboarders. The collection represents the main movements in art since 1945, mainly (but not exclusively) in Catalunya and Spain, and is shown in rotating exhibitions, so, depending on when you visit, you may catch works by major names such as Joan Miró or Antoni Tàpies, or coincide

▼ SKATEBOARDERS OUTSIDE MACBA

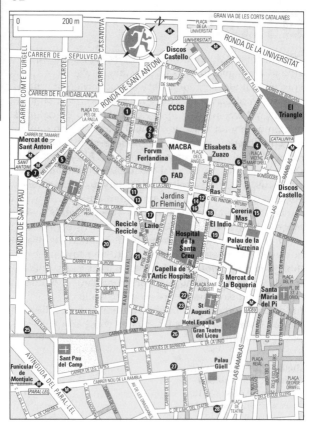

BARS AND CLUBS					
Almirall	3	Jazz Sí Club	5	Muy	
Bar Ra	19	Kabara	22	Buenas	17
Café de les		Llantiol	20	Paloma	1
Delícies	24	London Bar	27		
Confitería	25	Merry Ant	11		
Dostrece	18	Moog	28		
Fortuny	12	Muebles Navarro	13		

CAFÉS, TAPAS AND RESTAURANTS			
ànima	16	Granja M. Viader	15
Biblioteca	23	Kasparo	4
Casa de la		Mamacafé	9
Rioja	10	Pollo Rico	26
Elisabets	6	Sesamo	7
Fragua	21	Silenus	14
Granja de Gavà	2	Tres Tombs	8

with shows by contemporary Catalan conceptual artists. Probably the best way to acquaint yourself with the collection is to take the free guided tour (Wed & Sat at 6pm, Sun and public hols at noon). There's also a good museum shop, selling everything from designer espresso cups to art books, and a café around the back that's part of the CCCB (see p.83).

Foment de les Artes Décoratives (FAD)

Pl. dels Àngels 5–6 ☎934 437 520, ⊛www.fadweb.com. Tues–Fri 11am–8pm, Sun 11am–4pm. Free. Part of the former Convent dels

Àngels now houses the headquarters of the Foment de les Artes Décoratives (FAD) – a decorative art and design organization founded in 1903 – whose exhibition spaces (including the former convent chapel) are dedicated to industrial and graphic design, crafts, architecture, contemporary jewellery and fashion. Drop by to see the latest temporary exhibitions, or call in to frequent the spiffy bar and restaurant. FAD also coordinates the annual **Tallers Oberts** (or "Open Workshops"; last weekend of May and first weekend in June), when visitors can tour craft outlets in the Raval and Ribera.

Centre de Cultura Contemporània de Barcelona (CCCB)

C/Montalegre 5 ☎ 933 064 100, ⊛ www.cccb.org. Mid-June to mid-Sept Tues–Sat 11am– 8pm, Sun 11am–3pm; mid-Sept to mid-June Tues, Thurs & Fri 11am–2pm & 4–8pm, Wed & Sat

▼ SANT JORDI STATUE

11am–8pm, Sun 11am–7pm. Entry to exhibitions €4/5.50. The city's contemporary culture centre (CCCB) hosts temporary art and city-related exhibitions as well as supporting a cinema and a varied concert programme. The imaginatively restored building is a prime example of the juxtaposition of old and new; built as the Casa de la Caritat in 1714 on the site of a fourteenth-century Augustine convent, and added to in the late eighteenth and nineteenth centuries, it was for hundreds of years an infamous workhouse and lunatic asylum. In the entrance to the centre, in what is now called the Plaça de les Dones, you can see the old tile panels and facade in a patio presided over by a small statue of Sant Jordi, patron saint of Catalunya. At the back of the building the café (Mon–Fri 9am–7pm, Sat & Sun 11am–6pm) makes the most of its *terrassa* on the modern square joining the CCCB to the MACBA.

Plaça Vicenç Martorell

One of Barcelona's nicest traffic-free squares lies just off the Ramblas, a few minutes' walk from MACBA. There are not many places in the old town where children can play safely, so the small playground here (with swings and a slide) is all the more welcome for local families. What's more, it's overlooked by a first-rate café, the *Kasparo* (see p.87), whose arcade tables are busy from morning to night – a real find if you're looking for a break from sightseeing. Meanwhile, around the corner, the narrow **Carrer del Bonsuccés** and **Carrer dels Tallers** house a concentrated selection of the city's best independent music and CD stores.

Hospital de la Santa Creu

Entrances on c/del Carme and c/de l'Hospital. Daily 10am–dusk. Free. The district's most substantial historic relic is an attractive complex of Gothic buildings that was founded as the city's main hospital in 1402, a role it maintained until 1930. The spacious fifteenth-century hospital wards were subsequently converted for cultural and educational use, and now hold an artisanal school and two libraries, including the Catalan national library, the Biblioteca de Catalunya. Visitors can wander freely through the pleasant medieval cloistered garden (access from either street), while just inside the c/del Carme entrance (on the right) are some superb seventeenth-century decorative tiles and a Renaissance courtyard. The hospital's former chapel, **La Capella de l'Antic Hospital** (Tues–Sat noon–2pm & 4–8pm, Sun 11am–2pm; free), entered separately from c/de l'Hospital, is an exhibition space featuring a changing programme of works by young Barcelona artists.

Rambla de Raval

The most obvious manifestation of the changing character of El Raval is the palm-lined boulevard that has been gouged through the former tenements and alleys, providing a huge new pedestrianized area between c/de l'Hospital and c/de Sant Pau. The *rambla* has a distinct

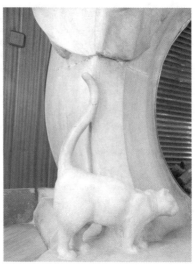

▲ DETAIL FROM HOTEL ESPAÑA

character that's all its own, dotted with kebab shops, halal butchers, telephone offices, neighbourhood bars and grocery stores, as well as an increasing number of rather fashionable cafés – a popular target for locals and tourists alike.

Just off the top of the *rambla* – tucked off c/de l'Hospital – the narrow **Carrer de la Riera Baixa** is at the centre of the city's second-hand/vintage clothing scene. A dozen funky little independent clothes shops and music stores provide the scope for an hour's browsing.

Hotel España

C/de Sant Pau 9–11 ☎933 181 758, ⊛www.hotelespanya.com. Some of the most influential names in Catalan *modernista* architecture and design came together at the turn of the twentieth century to transform the dowdy *España* hotel (originally built in 1860) into one of the city's most lavish addresses. With a tiled dining room designed by Domènech i

Montaner, a bar with an amazing marble fireplace by Eusebi Arnau, and a ballroom whose marine murals were executed by Ramon Casas, the hotel was the fashionable sensation of its day. It's been well looked after ever since, and you can have a good nosy around for the price of lunch or even stay here overnight – though the guest rooms are nowhere near as impressive as the public areas.

Palau Güell

C/Nou de la Rambla 3–5 ☎933 173 974. El Raval's outstanding building is the Palau Güell (1886–90), an extraordinary townhouse designed by the young Antoni Gaudí for wealthy industrialist Eusebi Güell i Bacigalupi. At a time when architects sought to conceal the iron supports within buildings, Gaudí turned them to his advantage, displaying them as decorative features in the grand rooms on the main floor, which are lined with dark marble hewn from the Güell family quarries. Columns, arches and ceilings are

all shaped, carved and twisted in an elaborate style that was to become the hallmark of Gaudí's later works, while the roof terrace culminates in a fantastical series of chimneys decorated with swirling patterns made from fragments of glazed tile, glass and earthenware. Unfortunately, guided tours of the building have been suspended whil rrenovation work is carried out, and Palau Güell is not expected to be open to the public until late 2006

Església de Sant Pau del Camp

C/de Sant Pau 101 ☎934 410 001. Mon–Fri 4.30–8pm, Sat 10am–2pm, Sun Mass at 10.30am & 12.30pm. €1. The name of the church of Sant Pau del Camp (St Paul of the Field) is a graphic reminder that it once stood in open fields beyond the city walls. The oldest and one of the most interesting churches in Barcelona, Sant Pau was a Benedictine foundation of the tenth century, built after its predecessor was destroyed in a Muslim raid of 985 AD, and constructed on a Greek cross plan. Above the main entrance are curious, primitive thirteenth-century carvings of fish, birds and faces, while other animal forms adorn the double capitals of the charming twelfth-century cloister. Inside, the church is dark and rather plain, enlivened only by tiny arrow-slit windows and small stained-glass circles high up in the central dome.

Mercat de Sant Antoni

C/del Comte d'Urgell 1 ☎934 234 287. Mon–Thurs & Sat 7am–2.30pm & 5.30–8.30pm, Fri 7am–8.30pm. The neighbourhood's major

▲ EGLÉSIA DE SANT PAU DEL CAMP

produce market makes a nice contrast to the Boqueria – there are not nearly so many tourists for a start – and, unlike many of the other city markets, it's surrounded by enclosed aisles packed with stalls selling cheap shoes, underwear, T-shirts, children's clothes, bed linen, towels and other household goods. Come on Sunday and there's a **book and coin market** (9am–2pm) instead, with collectors and enthusiasts getting here early to pick through the best bargains, from old paperbacks to commemorative coins. The traditional place to take a break from market shopping is *Els Tres Tombs*, the restaurant-bar across the road (see p.89).

Shops

Cerería Mas

C/del Carme 5 ☎933 470 138. Candles in every conceivable shape, design, size and colour.

Discos Castelló

C/del Tallers 3 ☎933 182 041; no.7 ☎933 025 946; and no.79 ☎933 013 575; ⊛www.discoscastello.es. Large music selection, with separate stores for classical recordings (no.3) and jazz and 70s pop-rock (no.79). No.7 is also a good place to buy concert tickets.

Forvm Ferlandina

C/Ferlandina 31 ☎934 418 018, ⊛www.forvmferlandina.com. Closed Sat pm, Mon & all Aug. Inventive, contemporary jewellery using a variety of design mediums.

Giménez & Zuazo

C/Elisabets 20 ☎934 123 381, ⊛www.gimenezzuazo.com. Two collections a year of cutting-edge women's fashion, funky and informal.

El Indio

C/del Carme 24 ☎933 175 442. The most traditional place in town to buy linen, pillows, blankets, sheets and tablecloths – the *modernista* facade, long cutting counters, wood panels and marble floor survive from its nineteenth-century glory days.

Lailo

C/de la Riera Baixa 20 ☎934 413 749. Second-hand and vintage clothes shop with a massively wide-ranging stock.

Ras

C/Dr Joaquim Dou 10 ☎934 127 199, ⊛www.actar.es. Opens 1pm, closed Mon. Specializes in books and magazines on graphic design, architecture and photography. Temporary exhibitions at the back are always worth a look.

Recicle Recicle

C/de la Riera Baixa 13 ☎934 431 815. Second-hand and vintage fashion, from the 1950s onwards, with a rapid turnover.

Cafés

Granja de Gavà

C/Joaquim Costa 37 ☎933 175 883. Mon–Fri 8am–1am, Sat 8am–2.30am. Traditionally tiled café with arty airs – witness the daubs on the walls, the 3m-high woman on the bar and the Wednesday-night poetry readings. Sandwiches, shakes, juices, crepes and salads served to an intellectual crowd.

Granja M. Viader

C/Xuclà 4–6 ☎933 183 486. Mon 5–8.45pm, Tues–Sat 9am–1.45pm & 5–8.45pm. The oldest *granja* (milk bar) in town, inventor of "Cacaolat" (a popular chocolate drink), but you could also try *mel i mató* (curd cheese and honey), *llet Mallorquina* (fresh milk with cinnamon and lemon rind) or a thick hot chocolate topped with fresh cream. A popular breakfast stop.

Kasparo

Pl. Vicenç Martorell 4 ☎ 933 022 072. Daily 9am–10pm, until midnight in summer; closed 2 weeks in Jan. Sited in the arcaded corner of a quiet square. There's muesli, Greek yoghurt and toast and jam for early birds. Later, sandwiches, tapas and assorted *platos del dia* (dishes of the day) are on offer – things like hummus and bread, vegetable quiche, couscous or pasta.

▲ SECOND-HAND CLOTHES STORE, C/DE LA RIERA BAIXA

Restaurants and tapas bars

ànima

C/dels Àngels 6 ☎ 933 424 912. Daily 1–4pm & 9pm–midnight. Funky joint attracting a young crowd, who come for the seasonally influenced fusion cooking – courgette flowers and mussels *tempura* followed by monkfish with a garlic and pistachio crust are typical summer dishes, with most mains around €14. It's a nice place for lunch, especially if you can get a table outside.

Biblioteca

C/Junta del Comerç 28 ☎ 934 126 261. Tues–Sat 1–4pm & 9pm–midnight; closed 2 weeks in Aug. One of the more agreeable of Barcelona's current dining hot spots – fish might be cooked Japanese- or Basque-style, clams paired with cured ham, lamb given the local treatment (with parsnip and turnip), or venison pie served with purée of the day. Meals cost around €35–40, though the €9 lunchtime *menú del dia* provides a more simple experience. Reservations advised.

Casa de la Rioja

C/Peu de la Creu 8–10 ☎ 934 433 363. Mon–Sat 1–4pm & 8–11pm; bar open from 9am and after 11pm. The Riojan Centre's contemporary-styled restaurant introduces Barcelona to the regional food of La Rioja, like *empedrado* (a potato, pork, pimiento and onion broth) or grilled *jurel* (a white fish) smothered in anchovy paste. The lunchtime *menú del dia* (€9.50) is an absolute steal, or the bar is open beyond meal times (and late) for excellent tapas.

Elisabets

C/d'Elisabets 2 ☎ 933 175 826. Mon–Fri 8am–midnight, Sat 8am–2am; closed Aug. Reliable Catalan home cooking at cramped tables in the brick-walled rear dining room (meals 1–4pm & 9pm–midnight), or tapas and drinks at the bar. The hearty €8 lunch is hard to beat, and there are set dinners and all-in tapas meals too.

Fragua

Rambla del Raval 15 ☏ 934 428 097. Tues–Sun 1–4pm & 8pm–1am. Classic old *bodega* with the smell of wood smoke in the air. Tables on the *rambla* are at a premium, though this is a cosy winter's day kind of place, too. Food is standard Catalan – lots of chargrilling (vegetables as well as meat and fish), tapas and a short vegetarian menu – and the prices are low, even discounting the €7 *menú del dia* (€10 at night).

Mamacafé

C/del Dr Joaquim Dou 10 ☏ 933 012 940. Mon–Sat 1pm–1am; open evenings only in Aug. It looks like a spruced-up boiler room but the modern Catalan food ("healthy and creative") is pretty good and the atmosphere laid-back. Mains cover everything from a house hamburger to salmon with Indonesian-style rice. There's a good value *menú del dia*, while outside meal times (1–4pm &

9pm–midnight) it operates as a café.

Pollo Rico

C/de Sant Pau 31 ☏ 934 413 184. Daily 10am–midnight. Barcelona's original "greasy spoon" has been here forever and, while it's not to everyone's taste, if you're in the mood for good spit-roast chicken, limp fries and a glass of rot-gut wine, served quick-smart at the bar, this is the place. The upstairs dining room is a tad more sophisticated (only a tad) – either way, you'll be hard pushed to spend €10 from a long menu of Spanish/Catalan staples.

Sesamo

C/Sant Antoni Abat 52 ☏ 934 416 411. Mon & Wed–Sat 1pm–1am, Sun 7pm–1am. Innovative yet inexpensive vegetarian cooking that will please the most discerning palate. The recipe: fresh, organic ingredients and influences from all over the globe. Meals are served 1pm to 3.30pm and 9pm till 11.30pm, with an €8 set lunch or a la carte dinner for under €20 – drop in for a drink at other times.

▼ SILENUS RESTAURANT

Silenus

C/dels Àngels 8 ☎ 933 022 680. Mon 1–4pm, Tues–Sat 1–4pm & 8.30–11.30pm. Very arty place near MACBA presenting some unique dishes – squid with broad beans and foie gras, for example, or even fillets of that well-known Catalan marsupial, the kangaroo. The interior is very Barcelona – distressed walls, leather banquettes, white tablecloths laid on marble tables. If you come for lunch you can eat from the *menú del dia* for around €10; otherwise, dinner costs at least €30.

▲ ELS TRES TOMBS

Els Tres Tombs

Ronda Sant Antoni 2 ☎ 934 434 111. Daily 6am–2am. Occupying a wide corner opposite the Mercat de Sant Antoni, this gregarious bar-cum-restaurant barely closes, welcoming a good-natured mix of market traders, locals, students and tourists. The food's good (there's a big selection of tapas), or you can just pull up a chair on the *terrassa* and soak up the street scenes.

Bars

Almirall

C/de Joaquin Costa 33 ☎ 933 189 917. Daily 7pm–3am. Dating from 1860, Barcelona's oldest bar – check out the *modernista* counter – is a venerated leftist hangout, not to mention a great

place to kick off a night's bar-hopping.

Bar Ra

Pl. de la Garduña 3 ☎ 933 014 163, ⊛ www.ratown.com. Mon–Sat 9am–2am. Extremely hip bar behind the Boqueria market, with a groove-ridden music policy and a sunny patio. It's not just for drinks – breakfasts are out of the ordinary, and there's eclectic world cuisine for lunch and dinner.

Café de les Delícies

Rambla de Raval 47 ☎ 934 415 714. Daily 6pm–2am. Typical of the neighbourhood, this doll's house of a bar attracts an arty crowd, who relax amid shelves of books and temporary exhibitions.

Confitería

C/de Sant Pau 128 ☎ 934 430 458. Daily 7pm–3am. This *modernista* bakery and sweet shop – carved wood bar, faded tile floor, murals, antique chandeliers – is now a popular meeting point, with a friendly, relaxed atmosphere.

Fortuny

C/Pintor Fortuny 31 ☎ 933 179 892. Tues–Sun 7pm–1.30am; closed 1 week in Aug. Step back to the 1970s in this easygoing retro bar, where there's always time to sit and chat. A few tables are set aside for diners, who can chow down on light Mediterranean dishes.

Kabara

C/Junta de Comerç 20 ☎ 626 774 405. Tues–Fri 1–4pm & 8pm–2am, Sat & Sun 8pm–3am; closed Aug. Blood-red arts scene bar and multicultural space, with odds-and-ends furniture, gigs most nights (singers, open-mike sessions, reggae bands) and a chilled-out atmosphere. Cheap food too, including a popular fondue.

London Bar

C/Nou de la Rambla 34 ☎933 185 261, ⊛www.londonbarbcn.com. Daily 7.30pm–4.30am; closed 2 weeks in Aug. Opened in 1910, this well-known *modernista* hangout attracts a mostly tourist clientele these days, but it's still worth looking in at least once. It puts on jazz, swing, blues or tango gigs most nights, the music starting at 12.30am.

Merry Ant

C/Peu de la Creu 23 ☎626 787 126. Tues, Wed & Sun 7pm–12.30am, Thurs–Sat 9pm–2am. Virtually unmarked brown barn doors open onto a DIY bodger's delight – bar, seats and tables have all been fashioned from cannibalized furniture and assorted junk-shop debris. It's all a bit studied, and fiendishly cool, but *La Hormiga Feliz* (the sign you might see on the door) has a certain eccentric charm.

Muebles Navarro

C/Riera Alta 4–6 ☎607 188 096. Tues–Thurs & Sun 6pm–midnight, Fri & Sat 6pm–3am; closed 2 weeks in Aug. Relax in one of the various rooms of a converted furniture store, hence the bar's name, "Navarro Furniture". A friendly place to have a drink, it also does tasty sandwiches and excellent cheesecake.

Muy Buenas

C/del Carme 63 ☎934 425 053. Tues–Sat 9am–3am. The Raval's nicest watering hole, with a hip, eager-to-please staff making things go with a swing. A long marble trough does duty as the bar, and the beer's pulled from antique beer taps.

Clubs

Dostrece

C/del Carme 40 ☎933 017 306, ⊛www.dostrece.net. Daily 11.30pm–4am. Small club under a stylish "upper Raval" bar-restaurant where local musicians and DJs take care of the ambience. Every night is different, though the crowd is always young and cool.

Jazz Sí Club

C/Requesens 2 ☎933 290 020, ⊛www.tallerdemusics.com. Every night from 9pm in this small club there's different music: inexpensive rock, blues and jam sessions, plus jazz, *son cubano* and flamenco.

Llantiol

C/Riereta 7 ☎933 299 009, ⊛www .llantiol.com. Closed Mon. Idiosyncratic cabaret club featuring mime, song, clowns, magic and dance. Shows (€9–12) normally begin at 9pm and 11pm (12.30am on Fri & Sat).

Moog

C/Arc del Teatre 3 ☎933 017 282, ⊛www.masimas.com. Daily 11.30pm–5am. Influential club playing techno, electro, drum 'n' bass, house, funk and soul to a cool, but up-for-it crowd.

La Paloma

C/Tigre 27 ☎933 016 897. Thurs–Sat 6pm–5am. Fabulous *modernista* ballroom where old and young alike are put through their rumba and cha-cha-cha steps from 6pm to 9.30pm. Then, after 11.30pm, DJs take their positions. Mainly electro and other current beats, though Saturday's 1980s night is a blast and there's a once-a-month punk party.

La Ribera and Sant Pere

The traditional highlights of the old artisans' quarter of La Ribera are the graceful church of Santa María del Mar and the Museu Picasso, the latter Barcelona's biggest single tourist attraction. More recently, the neighbourhood has also become the location of choice for designers and craftspeople, whose boutiques and workshops lend it an air of creativity. Art galleries and applied art museums occupy the medieval mansions of Carrer de Montcada – the neighbourhood's most handsome street – while the *barri* is at its most hip in the area around the Passeig del Born, whose cafés, restaurants and bars make it one of the city's premier nightlife centres. To the north, across Carrer de la Princesa, medieval Sant Pere is in the throes of development around its revamped market, though it's the neighbourhood's one remarkable building, the *modernista* Palau de la Música Catalana, that really warrants the diversion. For this, the nearest metro station is Urquinaona, while for everything else in La Ribera you can start from Metro Jaume I.

Palau de la Música Catalana

C/Sant Pere Més Alt ☎932 957 200, ⊛www.palaumusica.org. Box office open Mon–Sat 10am–9pm. Guided tours daily 10am–3.30pm, in English on the hour. €7. *Modernista* architect Domènech i Montaner's stupendous concert hall doesn't seem to have enough breathing space in the tiny street it faces. Built in 1908, the bare brick structure is smothered in tiles and mosaics, with the highly elaborate facade resting on three great columns, like elephant's legs. The dramatic tiled lobby provides a taster of the stunning interior, which incorporates a bulbous stained-glass skylight capping the second-storey auditorium – which contemporary critics claimed to be an engineering impossibility. Visitor numbers on the guided tours are limited and you'll have to book in advance, either in

▼ MUSEU DE LA XOCOLATA

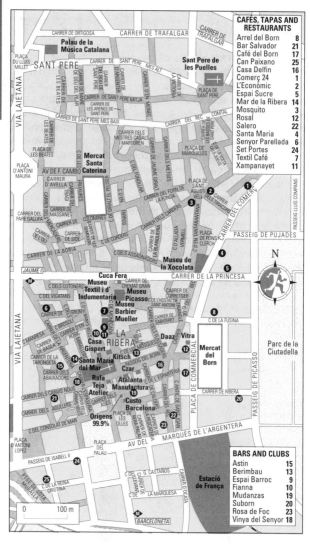

CAFÉS, TAPAS AND RESTAURANTS	
Arrel del Born	8
Bar Salvador	21
Café del Born	17
Can Paixano	25
Casa Delfín	16
Comerç 24	1
L'Econòmic	2
Espai Sucre	5
Mar de la Ribera	14
Mosquito	3
Rosal	12
Salero	22
Santa Maria	4
Senyor Parellada	6
Set Portes	24
Textil Café	7
Xampanyet	11

BARS AND CLUBS	
Astin	15
Berimbau	13
Espai Barroc	9
Fianna	10
Mudanzas	19
Suborn	20
Rosa de Foc	23
Vinya del Senyor	18

person or by phone at the box office, or by calling at the nearby gift shop, Les Muses del Palau, c/Sant Pere Mes Alt 1 (daily 9.30am–3pm). The concert season here (not all classical) runs from October to June and includes

performances by the Orfeó Català choral group and the Barcelona city orchestra, among others.

Església de Sant Pere de les Puelles

Pl. de Sant Pere ☎932 680 742.

▲ PICASSO T-SHIRTS

Mon–Sat 8.45am–1pm & 5–7.30pm, Sun 10am–2pm. Sant Pere's focal square is named, like the neighbourhood itself, for its monastic church, whose high walls and Gothic portal tower above the paved square's cast-iron drinking fountain. The church was rebuilt in 1147 on even older foundations, but has been restored inside over the centuries almost beyond interest. However, the three medieval streets that converge at the church, carrers de Sant Pere Més Alt (upper), Mitja (middle) and Baix (lower), contain the bulk of the district's finest buildings and the nicest shops – a mixture of small boutiques and old family businesses.

Mercat Santa Caterina

Avgda. Francesc Cambò 16 ☎ 933 195 740, ⓦ www.mercatsantacaterina.net. Work continues to spruce up the streets and squares around the mid-nineteenth-century Mercat Santa Caterina (also currently under restoration). The discovery of the foundations of a major medieval convent held up the market's renovation for a while, but it's expected to be open again to the public during 2005.

Museu de la Xocolata

C/del Comerç 36 ☎ 932 687 878, ⓦ www.museudelaxocolata.com. Mon & Wed–Sat 10am–7pm, Sun 10am–3pm. €3.80. Not many cities can boast a museum dedicated entirely to chocolate. Barcelona's is housed in the former Convent de Sant Agusti, whose thirteenth-century cloister, rediscovered when the building was renovated, can still be viewed. The museum itself recounts the history of chocolate, from its origins as a sacred and medicinal product of prehistoric Central America through to its introduction to Europe as a confection in the sixteenth century. As you might expect, the museum café serves a fine cup of hot chocolate – and the choccie counter is something to behold too – while at the adjacent Escola de Patisseria, glass windows allow you to look onto the students learning their craft in the kitchens.

Museu Picasso

C/de Montcada 15–23 ☎ 933 196 310, ⓦ www.museupicasso.bcn.es. Tues–Sat & hols 10am–8pm, Sun 10am–3pm. €5, first Sun of the month free. Despite containing none of his best-known works, Barcelona's Picasso Museum provides a unique opportunity to trace the artist's development from his paintings as a young boy to the mature works of later years. The early drawings, particularly, are fascinating, in which Picasso – still signing with his full name, Pablo Ruiz Picasso – attempted to copy the nature paintings in which his father specialized. Some works in the style of Toulouse-Lautrec, like the menu Picasso did for *Els Quatre Gats* tavern in 1900, reflect his interest in Parisian art; while other selected works are from the famous Blue Period (1901–04) and Pink Period (1904–06), and from his Cubist (1907–20) and Neoclassical (1920–25) stages. The large gaps in the main collection only underline Picasso's extraordinary changes of style and mood, best illustrated by the large jump to 1957, a year represented by his fifty-odd interpretations of Velázquez's masterpiece *Las Meninas*. The museum's minor works – sketches, drawings and prints – cover in detail most phases of the artist's career up until 1972, with the top floor incorporating various studies of Jacqueline, his wife.

A café with a *terrassa* in one of the courtyards offers refreshments, and there is of course a shop, stuffed full of Picasso-related gifts.

Museu Textil i d'Indumentaria

C/de Montcada 12–14 ☎933 104 516, ⓦwww.museutextil.bcn.es. Tues–Sat 10am–6pm, Sun 10am–3pm. €3.50, first Sun of the month free; ticket also valid for Pedralbes museums, see p.153. The fourteenth-century Palau de Lliò contains the extensive collections of the city's Textiles and Clothing Museum. Selected items, from late Roman fabrics to 1930s cocktail dresses, all beautifully presented, demonstrate the art and technique behind cloth-making, embroidery, lace and tapestry work. The upper floor concentrates on Spanish and Catalan designers of the 1970s to 1990s, with a room devoted to Pedro Rodríguez (1895–1990), the first *haut couture* designer to establish a studio in Barcelona. Special exhibitions at the museum are well regarded (for which there's

Picasso in Barcelona

Although born in Málaga, **Pablo Picasso** (1881–1973) spent much of his youth – from the age of 14 to 23 – in Barcelona. The time Picasso spent here encompassed the whole of his Blue Period (1901–04) and provided many of the formative influences on his art. Not far from the Museu Picasso you can still see many of the buildings in which Picasso lived and worked, notably the Escola de Belles Arts de Llotja (c/Consolat del Mar, near Estació de França), where his father taught drawing and where Picasso himself absorbed an academic training. The apartments where the family lived when they first arrived in Barcelona – Pg. d'Isabel II 4 and c/Reina Cristina 3, both near the Escola – can also be seen, though only from the outside, while Picasso's first real studio (in 1896) was located over on c/de la Plata at no.4. A few years later, many of his Blue Period works were finished at a studio at c/del Comerç 28. His first public exhibition was in 1901 at *Els Quatre Gats* tavern (c/Montsió 3, Barri Gòtic; ⓦwww.4gats.com); you can still have a meal there today.

▲ MUSEU TEXTIL I D'INDUMENTARIA

usually a separate charge), while the courtyard *Textil Café* (see p.97) is one of the nicest in the old town. In the associated shop, funky jewellery, silk ties, candles, kitchen aprons, bags and other design-led gifts and trinkets abound.

Museu Barbier-Mueller

C/de Montcada 14 ☎ 933 104 516. Tues–Sat 10am–6pm, Sun 10am–3pm. €3, first Sun of the month free. A fascinating collection of Pre-Columbian art is housed in the renovated sixteenth-century Palau Nadal, next door to the Textiles and Clothing Museum. The collection contains some beautiful pieces of sculpture, pottery, jewellery and textiles from early Mesoamerican cultures from Mexico to Peru. Afterwards, have a browse in the museum shop, which has a wide range of ethnic artefacts, from wall hangings and jewellery to terracotta pots and figurines. And if you're looking for a Panama hat, this is the place.

Església de Santa María del Mar

Pl. de Santa Maria 1, at Pg. del Born ☎ 933 102 390. Daily 9am–1.30pm & 4.30–8pm; Sun choral Mass at 1pm. The church was begun on the order of King Jaume II in 1324, and finished in only five years. Built on what was the seashore in the fourteenth century, Santa María was at the heart of the medieval city's maritime and trading district (c/Argentería, named after the silversmiths who worked there, still runs from the church square to the city walls of the Barri Gòtic), and it came to embody the commercial supremacy of the Crown of Aragon (of which Barcelona was capital). It's an exquisite example of Catalan-Gothic architecture, with a wide nave and high, narrow aisles, and for all its restrained exterior decoration is still much dearer to the heart of the average local than the cathedral, the only other church in the city with which it compares. The Baroque trappings were destroyed during the Civil War, which is probably all to the good since the long-term restoration work has concentrated on showing off the simple spaces of the interior; the stained glass, especially, is beautiful.

Behind the church is the square known as **Fossar de les Moreres**, which marks the spot

▲ SANTA MARÍA DEL MAR

cupola, is now empty, but works are underway to refit it as a public library. Boutiques and craft workshops hide in the narrow medieval alleys on either side of the *passeig* – carrers Flassaders and Vidreria, in particular, are noted for clothes, shoes, jewellery and design galleries. At night the Born becomes one of Barcelona's biggest bar zones, as spirited locals frequent a panoply of drinking haunts – from old-style cocktail lounges to thumping music bars.

where, following the defeat of Barcelona on September 11, 1714, Catalan martyrs fighting for independence against the King of Spain, Felipe V, were executed. A red steel scimitar with an eternal flame commemorates the fallen.

Passeig del Born

Fronting the church of Santa María del Mar is the fashionable Passeig del Born, once the site of medieval fairs and tournaments and now an avenue lined with a parade of plane trees shading a host of classy bars and shops. Cafés at the eastern end put out tables in front of the old Mercat del Born (1873–76), once the biggest of Barcelona's nineteenth-century city market halls. The massive rectangular steel and iron construction, topped with a perky little

Shops

Atalanta Manufactura

Pg. del Born 10 ☏932 683 702. Sells naturally dyed and painted silk and linen, including lovely scarves and wall hangings.

Casa Gispert

C/Sombrerers 23 ☏933 197 535, ⓦ www.casagispert.com. Roasters of nuts, coffee and spices for over 150 years – a truly delectable store with some tantalizing smells.

Cuca Fera

C/Cremat Gran 9 ☏932 683 710. Closed Mon am. Original children's clothing, from snazzy T-shirts to matching outfits.

Custo Barcelona

Pl. de les Olles 7 ☏932 687 893, ⓦ www.custo-barcelona.com. Where the stars get their T-shirts. Hugely colourful (and highly priced) designer Ts, tops and sweaters for men and women. Also at c/de Ferran 36 in the Barri Gòtic.

Czar

Pg. del Born 20 ☎933 107 222. A galaxy of running shoes, pumps, bowling shoes and baseball boots – if your Starsky and Hutch Adidas SL76s have worn out, they'll sell you another pair.

Daaz

C/Flassaders 27–29 ☎933 194 976. Pascal Frot designs furniture and lamps and is also responsible for the interior of various shops in Barcelona (including the very glam shoe shop opposite). Temporary exhibitions are held in his design gallery.

Kitsch

Pl. de Montcada 10 ☎933 195 768. Known for its papier-mâché models – matadors, flamenco dancers, pierrots and other characters – which are all unique. Also handmade paper fans.

Orígens 99.9%

C/Vidrieria 6–8 ☎933 107 531. An old stone arch divides the building, one side a deli-shop for wine, gourmet items and provisions, the other a tavern-bar for tasting typical Catalan dishes.

Rafa Teja Atelier

C/Santa Maria 18 ☎932 377 059. A browser's delight for gorgeous silk scarves, mohair wraps and Chinese-style silk jackets and dresses.

Vitra

Pl. Comercial 5 ☎932 687 219, ⓦwww.vitra.com. Home and workplace furniture specialist, with stunning chairs by the likes of Frank O. Gehry, Philippe Starck, Charles and Ray Eames, and Ron Arad.

Cafés

Café del Born

Pl. Comercial 10 ☎932 683 272. Mon–Thurs & Sun 9am–1am, Fri & Sat 9am–3.30am. No gimmicks, no dodgy art and no fusion food – just a successful neighbourhood café-bar with wooden floors, high ceiling and a simple Mediterranean menu. Sunday brunch is popular.

Rosal

Pg. del Born 27; no phone. Daily 9am–2am. The *terrassa* at the end of the Born gets the sun all day, making it a popular meeting place, though it's also packed on summer nights.

Textil Café

C/de Montcada 12–14 ☎932 682 598. Tues–Sun 10am–midnight. Set inside the shady, cobbled medieval courtyard of the Textile and Clothing Museum, this serves hummus, tzatziki, quiche, salads, chilli, lasagne and big sandwiches all day – or there's a €9.20 *menú del dia*.

Restaurants and tapas bars

Arrel del Born

C/Fusina 5 ☎933 199 299, ⓦwww.arreldelborn.com. Mon–Sat 1–4pm & 8.30pm–midnight, Sun 1–4pm. Lovely, light-filled restaurant with a warehouse-style interior. Fish is the speciality here, hand-caught by the owner's uncle, and if there's a rice dish on the menu choose it – it's always fantastic. Meals can easily top €40, though a *menú del dia* for around half this offers a cheaper way to enjoy the assured cooking. Dinner reservations advised.

Bar Salvador

C/dels Canvis Nous 8 ☎933 101 041. Mon–Fri 9am–5pm. Fillets of fish in egg batter, grilled steak with potato wedges, huge plates of *escalivada* (grilled aubergine, pepper and onion), or *botifarra* (sausage) with haricot beans are examples from a changing menu of half a dozen starters and mains and a few classic puds. Everything costs around €5, which is why tables are packed at lunch, but you shouldn't have to wait long.

Can Paixano

C/Reina Cristina 7 ☎933 100 839. Mon–Sat 9am–10.30pm. Unmarked stand-up bar (next to *Bazar Internacional*) where the only drink is champagne. Don't go thinking sophistication – it might come in traditional champagne saucers (the sort of thing Dean Martin used to stack in a pyramid and then pour wine over), but this is a counter-only joint where there's

▲ PASSEIG DEL BORN

fizz, tapas and sandwiches, and that's your lot.

Casa Delfin

Pg. del Born 36 ☎933 195 088. Mon–Sat 8am–5pm; closed Aug. Old-school paper-tablecloth bar-restaurant that offers a cheap and cheerful *menú del dia* – up to ten fish and ten meat choices, from grills to stews, topped off by home-made desserts or fruit. Add a coffee and the whole blowout shouldn't top €12.

Comerç 24

C/Comerç 24 ☎933 192 102, ⊛www.carlesabellan.com. Tues–Sat 1.30–3.30pm & 8.30pm–12.30am; closed 2 weeks in Aug. Chef Carles Abellan presents "glocal" cooking (ie global + local), dishes from across the world, interpreted locally by a master of invention. In an oh-so-cool interior, the meal comes tapas-style, mixing flavours and textures with seeming abandon but to calculated effect (*foie gras* and truffle hamburger, shot glasses of frothy soup, tuna *sashimi* on pizza). Prices are high (around €60 a head), but this is as good as contemporary dining in the city gets. Reservations advised.

L'Econòmic

Pl. de Sant Agusti Vell 13 ☎933 196 494. Mon–Fri 12.30–4.30pm; closed Aug. The beautifully tiled dining room dates back to 1932, and makes the perfect surroundings for a hearty lunch, served up, as the name implies, for a very reasonable price – around €9 for a three-course meal and wine. You may have to wait under the arches outside for a table to become available.

Espai Sucre

C/de la Princesa 53 ☎932 681 630, ⓦwww.espaisucre.com. Tues–Sat 9pm–midnight; closed Aug. The "Sugar Space" takes the current fad for food deconstruction off at a tangent by serving pretty much just dessert – inspired creations by Jordi Butrón, who assembles flavours and textures with the skill of a magician. There's a three-course (€21) or five-course (€32) seasonally changing pudding menu, with a small selection of savoury "mains" to pad out the experience.

Mar de la Ribera

C/Sombrerers 7 ☎933 151 336. Mon 8–11.30pm, Tues–Sat 1–4pm & 8–11.30pm. A cosy little place serving the best Galician-style seafood at prices (€5–10) that encourage large, leisurely meals. Try the mixed fried fish and paella, or any of the simple steaks and fillets – hake, salmon, tuna, sole, calamari – dressed with oil, garlic and chopped parsley, accompanied by platters of tasty grilled vegetables.

Mosquito

C/dels Carders 46 ☎932 687 569. Tues–Thurs & Sun 5pm–1am, Fri & Sat 5pm–2.30am. Delicious pan-Asian tapas, including Balinese chicken wings, Thai noodles and crispy spinach *pakoras*. Add friendly service, Fair Trade coffee, world music and very reasonable prices for a winning combination.

▼ MERCAT DEL BORN

Salero

C/Rec 60 ☎ 933 198 022. Mon–Fri
1–4pm & 9pm–midnight, Sat
9pm–midnight; closed 2 weeks in Aug.
Mediterranean cuisine with
subtle Asian touches, presenting
delights like an aubergine curry
with coconut or a *mee goreng*
(fried noodle) of the day, with
most dishes costing €8–10. It's a
crisp, modern space – if white is
your colour, you'll enjoy the
experience. It's also open from
9am Monday to Friday for cakes
and sandwiches. Dinner
reservations advised.

Santa Maria

C/Comerç 17 ☎ 933 151 227,
🖝 www.santamania.biz. Tues–Sat
1.30–3.30pm & 8.30pm–12.30am.
Paco Guzmán's new wave tapas
bar has a glass-fronted kitchen
turning out taste sensations –
like Catalan sushi, octopus
confit, yucca chips, or quail with
salsa. Under €40 a head should
see you right, finishing on a
high note with the famous
"Dracula" for dessert – a shot
glass of strawberry and vanilla
cream flavours that sets off
crackles in your head.

▼ ARTIST'S SHOP

Senyor Parellada

C/Argenteria 37 ☎ 933 105 094. Daily
1–4pm & 8.30pm–midnight. Utterly
gorgeous renovation of an
eighteenth-century building has
kept the arcaded interior and
splashed the walls yellow. Food
is Catalan through and through
– cuttlefish and cod, home-style
cabbage rolls, duck with figs, a
papillote of beans with herbs –
served from a long menu that
doesn't bother dividing starters
from mains. Most dishes cost
between €6 and €12, while
more than a dozen puds await
those who struggle through.

Set Portes

Pg. d'Isabel II 14 ☎ 933 192 950 or
933 193 033. Daily 1pm–1am. The
decor in the wood-panelled
"Seven Doors" has barely
changed in 150 years and, while
very elegant, it's not exclusive.
The rice dishes are famed and
are fairly reasonably priced
(€11–16), but for a full seafood
meal you're looking at around
€40 a head.

Xampanyet

C/de Montcada 22 ☎ 933 197 003.
Tues–Sat noon–4pm & 6.30–11pm,
Sun noon–4pm; closed Aug.
Traditional blue-tiled bar doing
a roaring trade in sparkling *cava*
and cider. Salted anchovies are
the house speciality, but there's
also marinaded tuna, spicy
mussels, sliced meats and cheese.
As is often the way, the drinks
are cheap and the tapas turn out
to be rather pricey, but there's
always a buzz about the place.

Bars

Berimbau

Pg. del Born 17 ☎ 933 195 378. Daily
6pm–2.30am. The oldest Brazilian
bar in town, still a great place

▲ PALAU DALMASES

for authentic sounds and killer cocktails.

Espai Barroc

Palau Dalmases, c/de Montcada 20 ☏933 100 673. Tues–Sat 8pm–2am, Sun 6–10pm. One of a series of handsome mansions along c/de Montcada, Palau Dalmases is open in the evenings as a rather grand bar, which could double as a Peter Greenaway film set. You can sip champagne or cognac in the refined surroundings or, once a week, enjoy live Baroque and chamber music (Thurs at 11pm; €18, drink included).

Fianna

C/Banys Vells 19 ☏933 151 810. Mon–Sat 7pm–2am, Sun 11am–8pm. Flickering candelabras, parchment lampshades, rough plaster walls and deep colours set the mood in this stylish Gothic mansion lounge-bar. Relax on cushions for a drink, or book ahead to eat – it's a popular weekend dinner and Sunday brunch spot.

Mudanzas

C/Vidrería 15 ☏933 191 137. Daily 10am–3am. Locals like the relaxed feel (especially if you can hide yourself away in the upper room), while those in the know come for the wide selection of rums from around the world.

Rosa de Foc

C/del Rec 69 ☏933 195 171, ⊛www.larosadefoc.com. Daily 6pm–2.30am. Multicultural space presenting exhibitions and live music, plus book launches, poetry readings and similar events. The spacious bar is usually quiet enough for a chat – at least, early on – and there are sandwiches and platters on the menu.

Vinya del Senyor

Pl. Santa Maria 5 ☏933 103 379. Mon–Thurs noon–1am, Fri & Sat noon–2am, Sun noon–midnight. Nook-and-cranny wine bar with tables right outside the lovely church of Santa María del Mar. The wine list runs to novel length – a score of them available by the glass – with oysters, smoked salmon and the like to wash it all down.

Clubs

Astin

C/Abaixadors 9 ☏933 010 090, ⊛www.nitsa.com/astin. Thurs–Sat 10pm–3am. Thumping bar-club for cutting-edge pop, house, techno and other beats. Live bands and guest DJs feature regularly – there's no point going until after midnight.

Suborn

C/de Ribera 18 ☏933 101 110. Tues–Sun 9.30pm–3am. A tapas and light meals place in the early evening (the *terrassa* overlooks Parc de la Ciutadella), which transforms itself into a club as the night wears on – the guest DJs spin just about everything.

Parc de la Ciutadella

For time out from the old town's historic intrigues and labyrinthine alleys, retreat to the city's favourite green space, Parc de la Ciutadella, on the eastern edge of La Ribera. It holds a full set of attractions – the Catalan parliament building (not open to the public), plant houses, museums and a zoo – though on lazy summer days there's little incentive to do any more than stroll the shady garden paths and pilot rowboats across the placid ornamental lake. The park dates from the demolition in 1869 of a Bourbon citadel, erected here in the mid-eighteenth century after Barcelona's resistance during the War of the Spanish Succession. Ciutadella was subsequently chosen as the site of the 1888 Universal Exhibition – from which period dates a series of buildings and monuments by the city's pioneering modernista architects. The park's main gates are on Passeig de Picasso (a short walk from La Ribera), and there's also an entrance on Passeig de Pujades (Metro Arc de Triomf); for direct access to the zoo, use Metro Ciutadella-Vila Olímpica.

Arc de Triomf

Pg. Lluís Companys. The giant brick arch at the northern end of Passeig Lluís Companys announces the architectural splendours to come in the Ciutadella park itself. Roman in

▼ ARC DE TRIOMF

scale, yet reinterpreted by its *modernista* architect, Josep Vilaseca i Casanovas, as a bold statement of Catalan intent, it's studded with ceramic figures and motifs and topped by two pairs of bulbous domes. The reliefs on the main facade show the city of Barcelona welcoming visitors to the 1888 Universal Exhibition, which was held in the park to the south.

Cascada

Parc de la Ciutadella. Park open daily 8am–dusk. Perhaps the most notable of the park's structures is the monumental fountain in the northeast corner. It was designed by Josep Fontseré i Mestrès, the architect chosen to oversee the conversion of the former citadel grounds into a park, and he was assisted by the young Antoni Gaudí, then a

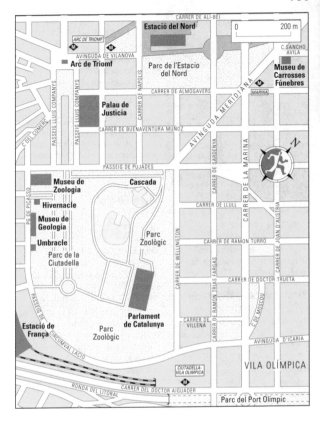

student: the Baroque extravagance of the Cascada's statuary (notably its dragons) is suggestive of the flamboyant decoration that was later to become Gaudí's trademark. The best place to contemplate the fountain's tiers and swirls is from the small open-air café just to the south. Here you'll also find a lake, where for a few euros you can rent a rowboat and paddle about among the ducks.

Museu de Zoologia

Pg. de Picasso ☎ 933 196 912, ⓦ www.museuzoologia.bcn.es. Tues, Wed & Fri–Sun 10am–2pm, Thurs 10am–6.30pm. €3, first Sun of the month free. The city's zoological museum presents a rather dry series of displays about Iberian fauna, though temporary exhibitions occasionally spark more interest. The building, however, is a different matter altogether, worth the admission fee alone – a red-brick, castle-like design by Domènech i Montaner, intended for use as the Universal Exhibition's café-restaurant. Dubbed the "Castell dels Tres Dragons", it became a centre for *modernista* arts and crafts, and many of Domènech's contemporaries spent time here

▲ MUSEU DE ZOOLOGICA

experimenting with new materials and refining their techniques.

Hivernacle and Umbracle

Pg. de Picasso. Both open daily 8am–dusk. Free. The two unsung glories of Ciutadella are its plant houses, arranged either side of the Geological Museum. The imposing Umbracle (palm-house) is a handsome structure with a barrelled wood-slat roof supported by cast-iron pillars, which allows shafts of light to play across the assembled palms and ferns. Both materials and concept are echoed in the larger Hivernacle (conservatory), whose enclosed greenhouses are separated by a soaring glass-roofed terrace. A refined café-bar at the Hivernacle (see p.105) is the best stop in the park for drinks or a meal.

Museu de Geologia

Pg. de Picasso ☎ 933 196 895, ⊛ www.bcn.es/museuciencies. Tues, Wed & Fri–Sun 10am–2pm, Thurs 10am–6.30pm. €3, first Sun of the month free. The first public museum in Barcelona was based on the geological bequest of Francesc Martorell i Peña, who gave his name to the city's Geological Museum, which opened in 1882. In many ways it's a period piece, with nineteenth-century cases of exhibits housed in a classical pedimented building. There are rocks and minerals on one side, and fossils on the other, with many of the exhibits found in Catalunya, from fluorescent rocks to mammoth bones.

Parc Zoològic

C/de Wellington ☎ 932 256 780, ⊛ www.zoobarcelona.com. Daily: May–Aug 9.30am–7.30pm; April & Sept 10am–7pm; March & Oct 10am–6pm; Nov–Feb 10am–5pm. €12.90. The city zoo takes up most of the southeastern part of the Parc de la Ciutadella. It's hugely popular with families, as there are mini-train and pony rides, a petting zoo and daily dolphin shows alongside the main animal attractions. These include the jungle bird aviary, permanent gorilla exhibition and comprehensive collection of reptiles, while notable endangered species found at the zoo include the Iberian wolf,

▼ ROWBOATS, PARC DE LA CIUTADELLA

▲ PARC DE LA CIUTADELLA

and big cats such as the Sri Lanka leopard, snow leopard and the Sumatran tiger. However, the zoo's days here in its current form are numbered – the powers that be perhaps having finally appreciated the irony of its juxtaposition next to the parliament building, and grown weary of explaining to visiting dignitaries the source of the strong smell pervading the area. There are advanced plans to move the marine animals to a new coastal zoo and wetlands area at the Diagonal Mar seashore at Besós.

Museu de Carrosses Fúnebres

C/Sancho de Ávila 2 ☎ 934 841 700. Mon–Fri 10am–1pm & 4–6pm, Sat & Sun 10am–1pm. Free. Present yourself at the front desk of the Serveis Funeraris (funerary services) de Barcelona (by the blue Banc Sabadell sign) for one of the city's more esoteric attractions. You'll be escorted into the bowels of the building and the lights will be thrown on to reveal a staggering set of 22 funerary carriages, each parked on its own cobbled stage, complete with ghostly attendants, horses and riders suspended in frozen animation. Used for city funeral processions from the end of the nineteenth century onwards, most of the carriages and hearses are extravagantly decorated in gilt, black or white. Old photographs show some of the carriages in use in the city's streets, while showcases highlight antique uniforms, mourning wear and formal riding gear.

Cafés

Hivernacle

Pg. de Picasso ☎ 932 954 017. Daily 10am–1am. A quiet, relaxing *terrassa* set amongst the palm trees inside the nineteenth-century glass conservatory. It's a genteel stop for daytime drinks, fancy tapas or moderately priced Catalan dining (weekday *menú del dia* €12), with live music and jazz nights a couple of times a week.

Montjuïc

You'll need to reserve at least a day to see Montjuïc, the steep hill and park rising over the city to the southwest. It takes its name from the Jewish community that once settled on its slopes, and there's been a castle on the heights since the mid-seventeenth century. But it's as a cultural leisure park that contemporary Montjuïc is positioned, anchored around the heavyweight art collections in the Museu Nacional d'Art de Catalunya (MNAC). This is supplemented by works in two other superb galleries, namely contemporary art in the Caixa Forum and that of the famous Catalan artist Joan Miró in the Fundació Joan Miró. In addition, there are several other minor museums on the hill plus the substantial open-air collections of the Poble Espanyol (Spanish Village), quite apart from the arenas associated with the 1992 Olympics. Metro Espanya provides easy access to Caixa Forum, Poble Espanyol and MNAC; the Trasbordador Aeri (cross-harbour cable car from Barceloneta) and Funicular de Montjuïc (from Metro Paral.lel) drop you a short walk from the Fundació Joan Miró; while the Olympic area can be reached by escalators behind MNAC.

Plaça d'Espanya

When Montjuïc was chosen as the site of the International Exhibition of 1929, its slopes were laid with gardens, terraces, fountains and monumental buildings. Gateway to the Exhibition was the vast Plaça d'Espanya, based on plans by noted architect Josep Puig i Cadalfach. Arranged around a huge Neoclassical fountain, the square is unlike any other in Barcelona, and a radical departure from the *modernisme* so in vogue elsewhere in the contemporary city. Striking twin towers, 47m high, stand at the foot of the imposing Avinguda de la Reina Maria Cristina, which heads up towards Montjuïc, the avenue lined by huge exhibition halls still used for trade fairs. At the end of the avenue monumental steps

(and modern escalators) ascend the hill to the Palau Nacional, past water cascades and under the flanking walls, busts and roofline "kiosks" of two grand Viennese-style pavilions.

Tren Turístic de Montjuïc

Pl. d'Espanya ☏ 934 156 020. Departures every 30min, 10am–8.30pm. April to mid-June Sat, Sun & hols only; mid-June to Oct daily. €3.20. Montjuïc's summer-season train-trolley leaves regularly from Plaça d'Espanya and runs to all the major sights on the hill, including the castle. The return trip lasts about an hour and your ticket allows you to complete the full circuit once, getting on and off where you like.

Font Màgica

Pl. de Carles Buigas. May–Sept

Thurs–Sun 8pm–midnight, music starts 9.30pm; Oct–April Fri & Sat only at 7pm & 8pm. On selected evenings, the fountain at the foot of the Montjuïc steps becomes the centrepiece of an impressive if slightly kitsch sound-and-light show – the sprays and sheets of brightly coloured water appear to dance to the strains of Holst and Abba.

Caixa Forum

Avgda. del Marquès de Comillas 6–8 Ⓣ 934 768 600, ⓦ www.fundacio.lacaixa .es. Tues–Sun 10am–8pm. Free. The former Casamarona textile factory (1911) at the foot of Montjuïc conceals a terrific arts and cultural centre. The exhibition halls were fashioned from the former factory

buildings, whose external structure was left untouched – original girders, pillars and stanchions, factory brickwork and crenellated walls appear at every turn. The Casamarona tower, etched in blue and yellow tiling, rises high above the walls, as readily recognizable as the huge Miró starfish logos emblazoned across the building. The centre's celebrated contemporary art collection focuses on the period from the 1980s to the present, with hundreds of artists represented, from Antoni Abad to Rachel Whiteread. Works are shown in partial rotation, along with temporary touring exhibitions, and there's also a library and resource centre, the Mediateca multimedia space,

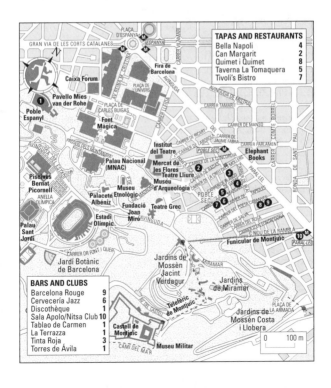

▲ PAVELLÓ MIES VAN DER ROHE

Poble Espanyol

Avgda. del Marquès de Comillas ☎935 086 330, ⊕www .poble-espanyol .com. Mon 9am–8pm, Tues–Thurs 9am–2am, Fri & Sat 9am–4am, Sun 9am– midnight. €7.

regular children's activities, and a 400-seat auditorium with a full programme of music, art, poetry and literary events. The café is a nice spot, too – an airy converted space within the old factory walls, serving sandwiches, snacks and lunch.

Pavelló Mies van der Rohe

Avgda. del Marquès de Comillas ☎934 234 016, ⊕www.miesbcn.com. Daily 10am–8pm. €3.50. The 1986 reconstruction by Catalan architects of the Pavelló Mies van der Rohe recalls part of the German contribution to the 1929 International Exhibition. Originally designed by Mies van der Rohe, and used as a reception room during the Exhibition, it's considered a major example of modern rationalist architecture. The pavilion has a startlingly beautiful conjunction of hard straight lines with watery surfaces, its dark-green polished onyx alternating with shining glass. It's open to visitors, but unless there's an exhibition in place (a fairly regular occurrence) there is little to see inside, though you can buy postcards and books from the small shop and debate quite how much you want a Mies mousepad or a "Less is More" T-shirt.

The Spanish Village – a hybrid open-air park of reconstructed famous or characteristic Spanish buildings – is the most extraordinary relic of the 1929 International Exhibition. "Get to know Spain in one hour" is what's promised and it's nowhere near as cheesy as you might think. It works well as a crash-course introduction to regional architecture – everything is well labelled and at least reasonably accurate. The echoing main square is lined with cafés, while the surrounding streets, alleys and buildings contain around forty workshops, where you can see engraving, weaving, pottery and other crafts. Inevitably, it's all one huge shopping experience – castanets to Lladró porcelain, religious icons to Barcelona soccer shirts – and prices are inflated, but children will love it (and you can let them run free as there's no traffic). Get to the village as it opens if you want to enjoy it in relatively crowd-free circumstances – once the tour groups arrive, it becomes a bit of a scrum. You could, of course, always come at the other end of the day, when the village transforms into a vibrant and exciting centre of Barcelona nightlife, its clubs (see p.116) among the hippest in the city.

Museu Nacional d'Art de Catalunya (MNAC)

Palau Nacional ☎ 936 220 376, ⓦ www.mnac.es. Tues–Sat 10am–7pm, Sun 10am–2.30pm. €4.80, first Thurs of the month free. Catalunya's national art gallery occupies the bulk of the towering Palau Nacional, set back on Montjuïc at the top of the long flight of steps from the fountains. It's one of Spain's great museums, combining a medieval art collection of international renown, as well as impressive holdings of European Renaissance and Baroque art, and nineteenth- and twentieth-century Catalan art (until the 1940s) – everything from the 1950s and later is covered by MACBA (see p.81). If time is limited it's recommended that you concentrate on the medieval collection, which is split into two main sections, one dedicated to Romanesque art and the other to Gothic – periods in which Catalunya's artists were pre-eminent in Spain.

The collection of Romanesque frescoes in particular is the museum's pride and joy, perhaps the best of its kind in the world. Removed from churches in the Catalan Pyrenees, they are presented in a reconstruction of their original setting, so you can see their size and where they would have been placed in the church buildings. Full explanatory notes (in English) cover the artistic techniques and iconography of the paintings, which for the most part, have a vibrant, raw quality, best exemplified by those taken from churches in the Boí valley. The evolution from the Romanesque to the Gothic period was marked by a move from mural painting to painting on wood, and the museum contains some outstanding altarpieces and church decoration as well as important works of the International Gothic or "1400" style, by artists like Jaume Huguet and Lluís Dalmau.

In the Renaissance and Baroque sections, major European artists from the fifteenth to eighteenth centuries are represented, though there are no real masterpieces. Instead, in a final flourish, it's MNAC's nineteenth- and twentieth-century Catalan art collection that stands out, particularly strong on *modernista* and *noucentista* painting and sculpture, the two dominant schools of the period.

Items from MNAC's more specialist collections of Catalan drawings, engravings, coins and photographs sometimes appear in temporary exhibitions on the lower level (separate entry €4.20, joint admission with main museum €6), which change every two to four months.

▼ POBLE ESPANYOL

Museu Etnològic

Pg. Santa Madrona 16–22 ☎ 934 246 402, ⍟ www.museuetnologic.bcn.es. Tues–Sun 10am–2pm. €3, first Sun of the month free. The Museu Etnològic boasts extensive cultural collections from Spain, Central and South America, Asia, Africa, Australia and the Middle East, housed in a series of glass hexagons. The collection itself is too big to exhibit at any one time, so the museum displays rotating exhibitions, which usually last for a year or two and focus on a particular subject or geographical area. The Spanish collections range across every province in the country, with exhibitions occasionally honing in on the minutiae of rural life and work, or examining medieval carving or early industrialization.

Museu d'Arqueològia

Pg. Santa Madrona 39–41 ☎ 934 246 577, ⍟ www.mac.es. Tues–Sat 9.30am–7pm, Sun 10am–2.30pm. €2.40. Montjuïc's archeological collection spans the centuries from the Stone Age to the time of the Visigoths, with the Roman and Greek periods particularly well represented. Finds from Catalunya's best-preserved archeological site – the Greek remains at Empúries on the Costa Brava – are particularly notable, and there's also an interesting selection of Iberian ceramics from around Catalunya and further south, including tablets bearing inscriptions in an ancient Iberian script, which is still indecipherable.

Teatre Grec

Pg. Santa Madrona 38 ☎ 933 161 000, ⍟ www.bcn.es/grec. Centrepiece of Barcelona's annual summer cultural Grec festival is this reproduction of a Greek theatre cut into a former quarry on the Montjuïc hillside. The festival starts in the last week of June (and runs throughout July and August), and incorporates drama, music and dance at a multitude of venues around the city – with some of the most atmospheric works performed here in the Greek theatre. Shows and events feature local unknowns to international superstars, and there's more information (and ticket bookings) at the Palau de la Virreina on the Ramblas (see p.53).

▼ POBLE SEC BALCONIES

La Ciutat del Teatre

Mercat de les Flors ☎934 261 875, ⊛www.mercatflors.com; Teatre Lliure ☎932 289 747, ⊛www.teatrelliure.com; Institut del Teatre ☎932 273 900, ⊛www.diba.es/iteatre. Downhill from the Palau Nacional, just to the east, steps descend the hillside to the theatre area known as La Ciutat del Teatre ("Theatre City"), which occupies a corner at the back of the old working-class neighbourhood of Poble Sec. The theatre buildings sit in a tight huddle off c/de Lleida, with the fringe-style **Mercat de les Flors** – once a flower market – and progressive **Teatre Lliure** ("Free Theatre") occupying the spaghetti-western-style Palau de l'Agricultura premises built for the 1929 Exhibition. Both have a full programme of theatre and dance, while Mercat de les Flors hosts an annual nonstop two-day performing arts festival (the Mataró de l'Espectacle, or "Entertainment Marathon") in June or July.

The sleek **Institut del Teatre**, meanwhile, brings together the city's major drama and dance schools, and various conservatories, libraries and study centres.

Poble Sec

The neighbourhood of Poble Sec, or "dry village" (so called because it had no water supply until the nineteenth century), is a complete contrast to the landscaped slopes of Montjuïc. There's nothing specific to see here, but the grid of steep streets is lined with down-to-earth grocery stores, bakeries, old-fashioned bars and good-value restaurants – the best eating places are listed at the end of this chapter. The neighbourhood has its own metro station, or it's an easy walk from El Raval, while the Montjuïc funicular (see p.112) has its lower station on the southern fringe of the neighbourhood at Metro Paral.lel.

Estadi Olímpic

Galeria Olímpica, Avgda. de l'Estadi ☎934 260 660, ⊛www.fundacio-barcelonaolimpica.es. April–Sept Mon–Fri 10am–2pm & 4–7pm; Oct–March Mon–Fri 10am–1pm & 4–6pm. €2.70. The 65,000-seater Olympic Stadium was the venue for the opening and closing ceremonies of the 1992 Barcelona Olympics. There's usually a gate open in the Neoclassical facade if you just want a glimpse of the pitch (the city's American football team, Barcelona Dragons, plays here, as does the other local soccer team, Espanyol). Olympics fans won't want to miss the stadium's **Galeria Olímpica**, which exhibits assorted items from the opening and closing ceremonies, and shows videos of the Games themselves.

In front of the stadium a vast *terrassa* provides one of the finest vantage points in the city. Long water-fed troughs break the concrete and marble expanse, while the confident, space-age curve of Santiago Calatrava's communications tower dominates the skyline.

Piscines Bernat Picornell

Avgda. de l'Estadi 30–40 ☎934 234 041, ⊛www.picornell.com. Mon–Fri 7am–midnight, Sat 7am–9pm, Sun 7.30am–4pm. €8. Remodelled and expanded for the Olympics, the city's favourite indoor swimming pools are open all year, while the outdoor pools are open to the public in summer only (June–Sept daily 9am–9pm). During the summer Grec festival, the pool hosts a

popular film-and-swim session –
one of Barcelona's more offbeat
cultural events.

Fundació Joan Miró

Parc de Montjuïc ☎934 439 470,
🌐www.bcn.fjmiro.es. Tues–Sat
10am–7pm, Thurs 10am–9.30pm, Sun
10am–2.30pm. €7.20, exhibitions
€3.60. Barcelona's most
adventurous art museum houses
the life's work of Joan Miró
(1893–1983), one of the greatest
Catalan artists, who established an
international reputation while
never severing his links with his
homeland. His friend, the
architect Josep-Luis Sert,
designed the impressive white
building set in lovely gardens
overlooking the city, inside which
is a permanent collection of
paintings, graphics, tapestries,
sculptures, sketches and notes,
most donated by Miró himself
and covering the period from
1914 to 1978. The paintings and
drawings in particular are
instantly recognizable, among the
chief links between Surrealism
and abstract art. Miró showed a
childlike delight in colours and
shapes and developed a free,
highly decorative style – you'll
notice his designs all over his
native city, most notably the
starfish logo of the savings bank,
Caixa de Pensions, and the
pavement mosaic in the middle
of the Ramblas. But darker works
on show reflect other passions,
like the fifty black-and-white
lithographs of the *Barcelona Series*
(1939–44), which encapsulate the
turmoil of the post-Civil War
period. The foundation also
displays works by other artists in
homage to Miró, with the single
most compelling exhibit being
Alexander Calder's Mercury
Fountain, which he built for the
Republican pavilion at the Paris

▲ COMMUNICATIONS TOWER, MONTJUÏC

Universal Exhibition of 1936–37
– the same exhibition for which
Picasso painted *Guernica*.

The museum lies just a few
minutes' walk from the Montjuïc
funicular and cable-car stations. It
sponsors excellent temporary
exhibitions, film shows, lectures
and children's theatre. There's also
a library, with books and
periodicals on contemporary art,
a bookshop selling posters, and a
café-restaurant (lunch 1.30–3pm,
otherwise drinks, pastries and
sandwiches) with outdoor tables
on a pleasant patio – you don't
have to pay to get into the
museum to use this.

Funicular de Montjuïc

Inside Metro Paral.lel, Avgda. del
Paral.lel ☎010, 🌐www.tmb.net. Every
10min daily 9am–10pm (Oct–March
until 8pm). €2.20 return. The
quickest way to reach the lower
heights of Montjuïc is to take
the funicular, which departs
from inside the station at Metro

Paral.lel and takes a couple of minutes to ascend the hill. At the upper station you can switch to the Montjuïc cable car (see below), or you're only a few minutes' walk from the Fundació Joan Miró.

Telefèric de Montjuïc

Avgda. de Miramar ☎010, ⑩ www.tmb.net. June to mid-Sept daily 11am–9pm; mid-Sept to Oct, April & May daily 11am–7pm; rest of the year weekends only 11am–7pm. €3.60 one-way, €5 return. The Montjuïc cable car whisks you up to the castle and back in little four-person gondolas, dangling passengers precariously over the landscaped grounds below. It's an exciting ride and the views, of course, are stupendous.

Jardins de Mossèn Costa i Llobera

C/de Miramar. Daily 10am–sunset. Free. The cross-harbour cable car from Barceloneta drops you close to a precipitous cactus garden which looks out over the port. Steep steps lead down into flourishing stands of Central and South American, Indian and African cacti, some over 6m high. It's a dramatic scene, little experienced by most visitors to Montjuïc, though the people lounging on the steps and in the shade of the bigger specimens suggest it's something of an open secret among the locals.

Castell de Montjuïc

Carretera de Montjuïc ☎933 298 613. Grounds: daily 7am–8pm; free. Museu Militar: mid-March to mid-Nov Tues–Sun 9.30am–8pm; mid-Nov to mid-March Tues–Sun 9.30am–5pm; €2.50. Built on seventeenth-century ruins, the castle's outer defences are constructed as a series of angular concentric perimeters, designed for artillery deflection, but the inner part is startlingly medieval in appearance, with its straight walls and square shape. The fort served as a military base and prison for many years after the Civil War, and it was here that the last president of the prewar Catalan government, Lluís Companys, was executed on Franco's orders on October 15, 1940. You can walk along the ramparts for free, and there's a little outdoor café within the walls. However, you have to pay to go inside the inner keep, where you'll find Barcelona's **Museu Militar**,

▼ CAFÉ AT FUNDACIÓ JOAN MIRÓ

containing an excellent collection of swords, armour, guns, medals, uniforms, maps and photographs.

Below the castle walls, a panoramic pathway – the **Camí del Mar** – has been cut from the cliff edge, providing scintillating views, first across to Port Olímpic and the northern beaches and then southwest as the path swings around the castle. The path is just over 1km long and ends at the back of the castle battlements, where a small house (open Sat & Sun only) sells drinks and rents out bikes for use on the surrounding wooded trails.

Jardí Botànic de Barcelona

C/Dr Font i Quer 2 ☎934 264 935, ⊛www .jardibotanic.bcn.es. Daily: April–June, Sept & Oct 10am–5pm; July, Aug & Nov–March 10am–3pm. €3. Principal among Montjuïc's many gardens is the city's Botanical Garden, laid out on the slopes behind the Olympic Stadium. Here, easy-to-follow paths wind through landscaped zones representing the flora of the Mediterranean, Canary Islands, California, Chile, South Africa and Australia. There are guided tours every weekend (except Aug) on the half-hour between 11am and 1.30pm.

Shops

Elephant Books

C/Creu dels Molers 12 ☎934 430 594, ⊛www.lfantbooks.4t.com. Only stocks English-language books, with cheap prices for current novels, classics, children's books and secondhand. A small café at the back serves English tea, home-made brownies, cakes and cookies.

▲ VIEW FROM CASTELL DE MONTJUÏC

Restaurants and tapas bars

Bella Napoli

C/Margarit 14 ☎934 425 056. Tues–Sun 1.30–4.30pm & 8.30pm–12.30am. Authentic Neapolitan pizzeria, right down to the cheery waiters and cheesy pop music. The pizzas – the best in the city – come straight from the depths of a beehive-shaped oven, or there's a huge range of pastas, risottos and veal *scaloppine*, with almost everything priced between €8 and €11. Be prepared to wait in line.

Can Margarit

C/Concòrdia 21 ☏ 934 416 723.
Mon–Sat evenings only, two sittings at
9pm & 11.30pm; closed Aug. This
rustic restaurant is extremely
popular with people wanting to
celebrate (every now and again
the lights will go off as a bottle
of champagne lit by a sparkler is
carried in). Help yourself to
wine from the barrels at the
entrance and eat easily for under
€20 – the rabbit (*conill*) with
caramelized onions and herbs is
a house speciality; otherwise it's
country salads, cured meats,
sausage and pork dishes.

Quimet i Quimet

C/Poeta Cabanyes 25 ☏ 934 423 142.
Tues–Sat noon–4pm & 7–11pm, Sun
noon–4pm. The neighbourhood's
nicest tapas joint, with a
chalkboard menu of twenty
wines by the glass and little
plates of food served from the
minuscule counter. Order a
roast onion, a marinaded
mushroom or two, stuffed
cherry tomatoes, grilled
aubergine and anchovy-
wrapped olives – classy finger
food for the discerning nibbler.

Taverna La Tomaquera

C/Margarit 58; no phone. Tues–Sat
1.30–3.45pm & 8.30–10.45pm, Sun
1.30–3.45pm. Sit down in this
chatter-filled tavern and the
bread arrives with a dish of olives
and two quail's eggs – and there
any delicacy ends, as the sweaty
chefs set to hacking steaks and
chops from great sides and ribs of
meat. The grilled chicken will be
the best you've ever had, and the
entrecôtes are enormous, while
the locals limber up with pan-
fried snails with *chorizo* and
tomato. Most main dishes cost
€6–11.

Tivoli's Bistro

C/Magalhaes 35 ☏ 934 414 017,
ⓦ www.tivolisbistro.com. Tues–Fri
8.30pm–midnight, Sat 1.30–4pm &
8.30pm–midnight; closed mid-Aug to
mid-Sept. Home-style Thai cuisine,
toned down for local tastes, but
reasonably priced and run by a
nice Catalan-Thai couple, who
also organize cooking classes. A
set meal (€18 per person, drinks
extra, dishes change monthly) is
delivered to your table, usually
incorporating a starter or two, a
red or green curry, a vegetable
and fish dish, and Thai noodles.

Bars

Barcelona Rouge

C/Poeta Cabanyes 21 ☏ 934 424 985.
Tues–Sat 11pm–3am. It's red all
right – couldn't be more red, in
fact, inside this laid-back

▼ JARDÍ BOTÀNIC DE BARCELONA

cocktail emporium playing downtempo jazz, trip-hop and other dreamy beats.

Cervecería Jazz

C/Margarit 43 ☎ 934 433 259. Mon–Sat 7pm–2.30am. Grab a stool at the carved bar and shoot the breeze over an imported beer in this amiable neighbourhood bar. The music policy embraces reggae and other mellow sounds, not just jazz.

Tinta Roja

C/Creu dels Molers 17 ☎ 934 433 243. Wed & Thurs 8pm–1.30am, Fri & Sat 8pm–2.30am, Sun 6–11pm. Highly theatrical tango bar with a succession of crimson rooms dripping with ornamentation leading through to a stage at the back. There's cabaret and live music (tango, rumba, Cuban) – often free – a couple of nights a week, though special shows are €10.

Clubs

Discothèque

Avgda. Marquès de Comillas, Poble Espanyol ☎ 934 231 285, ⊛ www.discothequebcn.com. Oct–May Fri & Sat midnight–7am. The winter destination for dedicated hedonists. Almost two thousand cram in here for house, garage, big-name DJs and a whole lot of style on the main dance floor.

Sala Apolo/Nitsa Club

C/Nou de la Rambla 113 ☎ 933 010 090, ⊛ www.nitsa.com. Regular live gigs with the occasional big name in an old-time ballroom setting. The techno/electronica *Nitsa Club* kicks off at weekends (Fri & Sat 12.30pm–6.30am) with guest DJs playing pumping sounds.

Tablao de Carmen

Avgda. Marquès de Comillas, Poble Espanyol ☎ 933 256 895, ⊛ www.tablaodecarmen.com. Tues–Sun from 9.30pm. The Poble Espanyol's long-standing flamenco club features a variety of styles and performers. Prices start at €30 for the show and a drink, rising to €55 and upwards for the show plus dinner. Advance reservations required.

Terrazza

Avgda. Marquès de Comillas, Poble Espanyol ☎ 934 231 285, ⊛ www.nightsungroup.com. May–Oct Thurs–Sun midnight–6am. Open-air summer club that's *the* place to be. Nonstop dance, house and techno, though don't get there until at least 3am and be prepared for the style police.

Torres de Ávila

Avgda. Marquès de Comillas, Poble Espanyol ☎ 934 249 309. Thurs–Sat midnight–6am. Located inside the mock-twelfth-century gateway in the "Spanish Village", this is a stunning fantasy of a dance club, with a fabulous panoramic terrace.

Port Olímpic and Poble Nou

The main waterfront legacy of the 1992 Olympics was the Port Olímpic, the sparkling marina development which lies fifteen minutes' walk along the promenade from Barceloneta. Locals have taken to this in a big way, making full use of the surrounding beaches and boardwalks, and descending in force at the weekends for a leisurely lunch or late drink in one of the scores of restaurants and bars. It's a pattern beginning to be repeated further north in the old working-class neighbourhood of Poble Nou, which overlays its traditional character with the buzz provided by one of Barcelona's hottest club scenes. There are metro stations at Ciutadella-Vila Olímpica and Poble Nou, or bus #59 runs from the Ramblas through Barceloneta and out to the Port Olímpic.

Port Olímpic

From any point along the Passeig Marítim, the soaring twin towers of the Olympic port impose themselves upon the skyline, while a shimmering golden mirage above the promenade slowly reveals itself to be a huge **copper fish** (courtesy of North American Frank Gehry, architect of the Bilbao Guggenheim). These are the showpiece manifestations of the huge seafront development constructed for the 1992 Olympics, which incorporated an athletes' village for the 15,000 competitors and support staff – the apartment buildings and residential complexes were converted into permanent housing after the Games. The port itself – site of many of the Olympic watersports events – is backed by the city's two tallest buildings, the **Torre Mapfre** and the steel-framed **Hotel Arts Barcelona**, both

154m high. Two wharves contain the bulk of the action: the Moll de Mestral has a lower deck by the marina lined with bars and *terrassas*, while the Moll de Gregal sports a double-decker tier of seafood restaurants.

Centre Municipal de Vela

Moll de Gregal, Port Olímpic ☎932 257 940, ◉www.vela-barcelona.com. Office open Mon–Fri 9am–9pm, Sat & Sun 9am–8pm. Sails often flit across the sparkling waters, as yachties and windsurfers take full advantage of the blue skies and breezes. If you fancy joining them, instruction in catamaran/laser sailing, kayaking and windsurfing is available from the Port Olímpic's sailing club. Prices vary considerably, but you can expect to pay around €30 for a couple of hours' windsurfing or €180 for a two-day elementary sailing course.

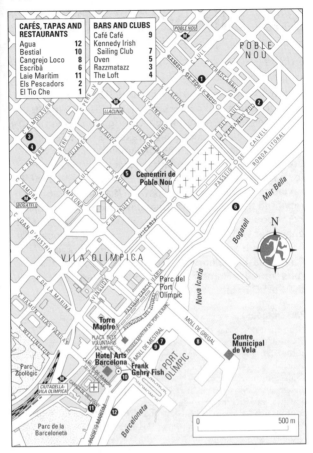

CAFÉS, TAPAS AND RESTAURANTS

Agua	12
Bestial	10
Cangrejo Loco	8
Escribà	6
Laie Marítim	11
Els Pescadors	2
El Tio Che	1

BARS AND CLUBS

Café Café	9
Kennedy Irish Sailing Club	7
Oven	5
Razzmatazz	3
The Loft	4

Rambla de Poble Nou

Pretty, traffic-free, tree-lined Rambla de Poble Nou runs inland through the most attractive part of nineteenth-century Poble Nou ("New Village") and is entirely modest in character – just a run of neighbourhood shops and cafés frequented by locals out for their daily stroll. Stop off for a cold drink at *El Tio Che* (see opposite) or lunch at *Els Pescadors* (p.121) – the metro (yellow line 4) will save you the walk back to Ciutadella, Barceloneta or the city centre.

Cementiri de Poble Nou

Avgda. d'Icaria. Daily 8am–6pm. This vast nineteenth-century mausoleum has its tombs set in walls 7m high, tended by families who have to climb great stepladders to reach the uppermost tiers. With traffic noise muted by the high walls, and birdsong accompanying a stroll around the flower-lined pavements, quiet courtyards and chapels, this village of the dead is a rare haven of peace in the city.

▲ RAMBLA DE POBLE NOU

locals en masse, while weekends see scratch games of beach volleyball and football played up and down the coast. Save your swim for a pool, though – while the sands are regularly swept and replenished, the sea water's still not as clean as it could be.

Cafés

Laie Marítim

Pg. Marítim 35 ☎932 247 173, ☜www.laie.es. Mon–Sat 8am–9.30pm, Sun 8.30am–5pm. This outpost of the *Laie* bookshop café, attached to the Poliesportiu Marítim sports centre, is a bit of a find amidst the chain bars and pricey restaurants – two minutes from the beach, with a sunny *terrassa*, great coffee, tapas and sandwiches, and a salad bar and light meals at lunch.

El Tio Che

Rambla Poble Nou 44–46 ☎933 091 872. Daily 10am–midnight; reduced hours in winter. Famous old *orxateria* in a down-to-earth

City beaches

A series of city beaches reaches north from the Port Olímpic, along a five-kilometre stretch of sandy coast as far the River Besòs. Split into different named sections (Nova Icària, Bogatell, etc), they are all furnished with boardwalks, showers and water fountains, while some also feature climbing frames, public art and open-air cafés. The merest hint of sun brings out the

Urban renewal

Since the early 1990s the transformation of Poble Nou and its near neighbours has formed part of an overall scheme to turn the 5km of shoreline from Barceloneta to the River Besòs into a high-tech business, leisure and residential corridor. The extension of Avinguda Diagonal to the sea, north of Poble Nou, provided the necessary rebranding, and it's as **Diagonal Mar** that the area hopes to prosper. Development was further boosted by Barcelona's Universal Forum of Cultures (held from May to September 2004), a sort of cultural and environmental Expo, which brought new amenities in its wake, including a convention centre, marina, beach, business district, university campus and metro and tram link. What attraction this development will have for tourists in the future is still to be seen, though it can't be denied that it's on a grand scale: the convention centre is the biggest in southern Europe, while the boast about the main Forum open space – the Plaza – is that it's the second largest square in the world (150,000 square metres) after Beijing's Tiananmen Square.

neighbourhood. Orange or lemon *granissat* (crushed-ice) and *orxata* (milky tiger-nut drink) come in various servings up to a litre, and there are also *torrons* (almond fudge), hot chocolate, coffee, croissants and sandwiches.

Restaurants and tapas bars

Agua

Pg. Marítim 30 ☎932 251 272, ⓦwww.aguadeltragaluz.com. Daily 1.30–4pm & 8.30pm–midnight, Fri & Sat until 1am. Depending on your mood (or the weather) you can choose the sleek, split-level dining room or seafront boardwalk garden. It's a contemporary Mediterranean menu – rice with quail, asparagus and mushroom, or grilled tuna *sofrito* (caramelized onions and tomato) – but the house hamburger figures too, alongside a short selection of tapas, pastas and salads. The prices are pretty fair (meals around €25), so it's usually busy.

Bestial

C/Ramon Trias Fargas 2–4 ☎932 240 407, ⓦwww.bestialdetragaluz.com. Daily 1.30–4pm & 8.30pm–midnight, Sat & Sun until 1am. Right beside Frank Gehry's fish (under the

wooden bridge) you'll find a pleasant terrace-garden in front of the beach, great for lunch. Inside, the feel is sharp and minimalist, while the cooking's Mediterranean, mainly Italian, with dishes given an original twist. Rice, pasta and wood-fired pizzas are in the €9–13 range, with other dishes up to €18. At weekends, you can drink at the bar until 2am.

Cangrejo Loco

Moll de Gregal 29–30 ☎932 210 533. Daily 1pm–1am. The large outdoor terrace or huge picture windows at the "Crazy Crab" offer panoramas of the local coast and marina. The fish and shellfish are first-rate, with the catch changing daily, but a mixed fried-fish plate or broad beans with prawns are typically Catalan starters. Paella can be thoroughly recommended too, and the service is spot-on. Around €30 and upwards.

Escribà

Ronda del Litoral 42, Platja Bogatell ☎932 210 729. Tues–Sat 11am–1am, Sun 11am–4pm; restricted hours in winter. Glorified beach shack – a *xiringuito* in the parlance – that's enough off the beaten track (a 20min walk along the prom from the Port Olímpic to mark you out as in the know. A tapas tasting plate for two is popular, and the paellas and *fideuàs* (from €12) fly out of the kitchen; daily fish specials are more like €20, and there's a ten percent terrace surcharge, but what the hell, the food and views are great.

▼ CEMENTIRI DE POBLE NOU

▲ VILA OLÍMPICA HOUSING

Els Pescadors

Pl. Prim 1 ☎ 932 252 018. Daily 1–4pm & 8pm–midnight. Considered something of a pilgrimage for fish-lovers (reservations advised), a meal here should certainly include a house special *fideuà* (noodles) or a Catalan classic like cod with *samfaina* (ratatouille) – though that's only just scratching the surface of a wide-ranging menu. If you don't go mad, you'll escape for about €50. The restaurant is hidden away in a pretty square in the back alleys of Rambla de Poble Nou.

Bars

Café Café

Moll de Mestral 30 ☎ 932 210 019. Mon–Thurs & Sun 3pm–3am, Fri & Sat 3pm–5am. Most of the Port Olímpic bars are indistinguishable – pumping sounds, backdrop video screens and preening youth – but *Café Café* is one of the few that dares to be different. It's more relaxed than the others, with a cane-chair colonial feel, and serves lots more besides coffee.

Kennedy Irish Sailing Club

Moll de Mestral 26–27 ☎ 932 210 039, ⊛ www.kennedybcn.com. Daily 6pm–5am. Barcelona's "little bit of Ireland" provides a beer drinkers' haven between the disco bars. Guinness and Murphy's on tap, plus live music (pub rock, covers, Irish) Thursday to Sunday and big-screen sports.

Clubs

The Loft

C/Pamplona 88 ☎ 933 208 200, ⊛ www.theloftclub.com. Fri & Sat 1–6am. Two dance floors (*The Loft* and *Lolita*) located in an old warehouse that form part of the *Razzmatazz* setup (see below). Resident and international DJs offer up a wide range of beats, from techno and electronica to Spanish pop. It's cheaper, or can be free before 2am (otherwise €12), but no one really turns up that early.

Oven

C/Ramon Turró 126 ☎ 932 210 602, ⊛ www.oven.ws. Mon–Fri 1.30pm–2am, Sat 6pm–2am; restaurant open Mon–Fri 1.30–4pm & 9–11.30pm, Sat 9pm–12.30am. Fabulously designed bar/club/restaurant occupying former factory premises. Lounge room at the front, restaurant at the back with a stunning open kitchen, and live music a couple of nights a week. After midnight the place turns into a club, with DJs until 2am or later.

Razzmatazz

C/dels Almogavers 122 ☎ 932 720 910, ⊛ www.salarazzmatazz.com. Fri & Sat 11pm–5am. *Razzmatazz* hosts the biggest in-town rock gigs at weekends, after which the *Razz Club* takes over – "three clubs in one" spinning indie, rock, pop, electro, Sixties and more. Entrance to all the bars and clubs, plus one drink, is usually €12.

Dreta de l'Eixample

The gridded nineteenth-century new-town area north of Plaça de Catalunya is the city's main shopping and business district. It was designed as part of a revolutionary urban plan – the Eixample in Catalan ("Extension" or "Widening") – that divided districts into regular blocks, whose characteristic wide streets and shaved corners survive today. Two parallel avenues, Passeig de Gràcia and Rambla de Catalunya, are the backbone of the Eixample, with everything to the east known as the Dreta de l'Eixample (the right-hand side). It's here, above all, that the bulk of the city's famous *modernista* (Catalan Art Nouveau) buildings are found, whose fanciful flourishes provide some of the most compelling urban images in Europe. However, any visit might equally concentrate on the Dreta's other undoubted pleasures – from museum and gallery visits to browsing in some of the city's most stylish shops. Start your exploration from either Metro Passeig de Gràcia or Metro Diagonal.

Casa Calvet

C/de Casp 48. Antoni Gaudí's earliest commissioned town-house building, erected for a prominent local textile family, dates from 1899 and, though fairly conventional in style, the Baroque inspiration on display in the sculpted facade and lobby was to surface again in his later, more elaborate buildings on Passeig de Gràcia. If you want a closer look inside, you'll have to book a table in the restaurant (see p.130) that now occupies the premises.

Passeig de Gràcia

The prominent showy avenue which runs northwest from

Modernisme

Modernisme, the Catalan offshoot of Art Nouveau, was the expression of a renewed upsurge in Catalan nationalism in the 1870s. Its most famous architectural exponent was **Antoni Gaudí i Cornet** (1852–1926), whose buildings are apparently lunatic flights of fantasy that at the same time are perfectly functional. His architectural influences were Moorish and Gothic, while he embellished his work with elements from the natural world. The imaginative impetus he provided to the movement was incalculable, inspiring other Catalan architects like **Lluís Domènech i Montaner** (1850–1923) – perhaps the greatest *modernista* architect – and **Josep Puig i Cadafalch** (1867–1957). It was in Domènech's café-restaurant at the Parc de la Ciutadella that a craft workshop was set up after the Universal Exhibition of 1888, giving Barcelona's *modernista* architects the opportunity to experiment with ceramic tiles, ironwork, stained glass and decorative stone carving. This combination of traditional methods with experiments in modern technology was to become the hallmark of *modernisme* – a marriage that produced some of the most fantastic and exciting modern architecture to be found anywhere in the world.

BARS AND CLUBS

Cervesera Artesana	1
Les Gens Que J'aime	9
Mond Club	2

CAFÉS, TAPAS AND RESTAURANTS

ba-ba-reeba	14
Bodegueta	6
Casa Calvet	19
Ciudad Condal	15
East 47	8
Forn de Sant Jaume	11
Japonés	3
Laie Llibreria Café	17
Muscleria	7
Mussol	10, 18
O'Nabo de Lugo	5
Thai Gardens	13
Tragaluz	4
Tramoia	16
Valor	12

Plaça de Catalunya as far as the southern reaches of Gràcia was laid out in its present form in 1827. As the Eixample became *the* fashionable part of town in which to live in the nineteenth century, the avenue developed as a showcase for the talents of *modernista* architects who were eagerly commissioned by status-conscious merchants and businessmen. Walk the length of Passeig de Gràcia from Plaça de Catalunya to Avinguda Diagonal (a 25min stroll) and you'll pass some of the city's most extraordinary architecture, notably the famous group of three buildings (casas Lleó Morera, Amatller and Batlló) known as the Mansana de la Discòrdia, or "Block of Discord", as they show off wildly varying manifestations of the *modernista* style and spirit. Further up is Antoni Gaudí's iconic apartment building La Pedrera while, in between, wrought-iron Art Nouveau street lamps, fashion stores, classy tapas bars and a designer hotel or two set the tone for this resolutely upscale avenue.

Casa Lleó Morera

Pg. de Gràcia 35. No public access.
Domènech i Montaner's Casa Lleó Morera (1906) is the least extravagant of the buildings in the so-called Mansana de la Discòrdia and has suffered more than the others from "improvements" wrought by subsequent owners, which included removing the ground-floor arches and sculptures. A Loewe leather clothes and accessories store occupies the ground floor, while the main entrance to the building is resolutely guarded to prevent more than a peek inside. This is a pity because it has a rich Art Nouveau interior, flush with

▼ CASA CALVET

▲ PASSEIG DE GRÀCIA

ceramics and exquisite stained glass, while its semicircular jutting balconies are quite distinctive.

Museu del Perfum

Pg. de Gràcia 39 ☎ 932 160 121, ⓦ www.museodelperfume.com. Mon–Fri 10.30am–1.30pm & 4.30–8pm, Sat 11am–2pm. Free.
They may have to turn the lights on for you at the back of the Regia perfume store, but there's no missing the exhibits as a rather cloying pong exudes from the room. It's a private collection of over five thousand perfume and essence bottles from Egyptian times onwards, and there are some exquisite pieces displayed, including Turkish filigree-and-crystal ware and bronze and silver Indian elephant flasks. More modern times are represented by scents made for Brigitte Bardot, Grace Kelly and Elizabeth Taylor, and if you're diligent enough to scan all the shelves you might be able to track down the perfume bottle designed by Salvador Dalí.

Casa Amatller

Pg. de Gràcia 41 ☎ 934 880 139. Mon–Sat 10am–7pm, Sun 10am–2pm. Free. Puig i Cadafalch's striking

Casa Amatller (1900) was created largely from the bones of an existing building and paid for by Antoni Amatller, a Catalan chocolate manufacturer. The facade rises in steps to a point, studded with coloured ceramic decoration and with heraldic sculptures over the doors and windows. Inside the hallway the ceramic tiles continue along the walls, while twisted stone columns are interspersed by

▼ MUSEU DEL PERFUM

dragon lamps, all of which is further illuminated by fine stained-glass doors and an interior glass roof. The ground floor contains the small **Centre del Modernisme**, which is worth calling in to to peruse its temporary exhibitions on the buildings and personalities of the *modernista* period. There's also an excellent selection of postcards for sale, while you can buy the useful *Ruta del Modernisme* ticket here (see p.188), which includes a free tour giving some background to the Mansana de la Discòrdia buildings.

Casa Batlló

Pg. de Gràcia 43 ☎932 160 306, ⓦwww.casabatllo.es. Daily 9am–2pm; also open some afternoons until 8pm. Visits to main/ground floors €10, attic/roof €10, both €16. Perhaps the most extraordinary creation on the "Block of Discord" is the Casa Batlló, designed for the industrialist Josep Batlló and finished in 1907. Antoni Gaudí contrived to create an undulating facade here that Salvador Dalí later compared to "the tranquil waters of a lake". There's an animal aspect at work too: the stone facade hangs in folds, like skin and, from below, the twisted balcony railings resemble malevolent eyes. The higher part of the facade is less abstruse and more decorative, pockmarked with circular ceramic buttons laid on a bright mosaic background and finished with a little tower topped with a cross. Self-guided audio tours show you the main floor, patio, attic and roof chimneys. It's best to reserve a ticket in advance (by phone or in person), as this is a very popular attraction.

Fundació Antoni Tàpies

C/Aragó 255 ☎934 870 315, ⓦwww.fundaciotapies.org. Tues–Sun 10am–8pm. €4.20. Housed in *modernista* architect Domènech i Montaner's first important building, the Casa Montaner i Simon (1880), is the definitive collection of the work of Catalan abstract artist Antoni Tàpies i Puig. You can't miss the foundation building – it's capped by Tàpies' own striking sculpture, *Núvol i Cadira* ("Cloud and Chair": 1990), a tangle of glass, wire and aluminium. The artist was born in Barcelona in 1923 and was a founding member (1948) of the influential avant-garde Dau al Set ("Die at Seven") grouping of seven artists. After a brief Surreal phase, Tàpies found his feet with an abstract style that matured in the 1950s, with underlying messages and themes signalled by the inclusion of everyday objects and symbols on the canvas. He has also continually experimented with unusual materials, like oil paint mixed with crushed marble, or employing sand, cloth or straw in his collages. Temporary exhibitions focus on selections of Tàpies' life's work, while the foundation also includes a collection of works by other contemporary artists.

Museu Egipci de Barcelona

C/de València 284 ☎ 934 880 188, ⊛ www.fundclos.com. Mon–Sat 10am–8pm, Sun 10am–2pm. €5.50, joint admission with Fundació Francisco Godia €8.50. Guided tours every Sat at noon & 6pm, included in admission. Barcelona's Egyptian Museum is an exceptional private collection of artefacts from ancient Egypt, ranging from the earliest kingdoms to the era of Cleopatra. It was founded by hotelier Jordi Clos – whose *Hotel Claris*, a block away, still has its own private museum for guests – and displays a remarkable gathering of over six hundred objects, amulets to sarcophagi. The emphasis is on the shape and character of Egyptian society, and visitors are given a hugely detailed English-language guidebook covering every item. But the real pleasure here is a serendipitous wander, turning up items like a wood-and-leather bed of the First and Second Dynasties (2920–2649 BC), some examples of cat mummies of the Late Period (715–332 BC) or a rare figurine of a spoonbill (ibis) representing an Egyptian god. There are temporary exhibitions, a library and a good book and gift shop on the lower floor, and a terrace café upstairs. The museum also hosts a full programme of study sessions,

children's activities and evening events – the reception desk can provide details.

Fundació Francisco Godia

C/de València 284 ☎ 932 723 180, ⊛ www.fundacionfgodia.org. Daily except Tues 10am–8pm. €4.50, joint admission with Museu Egipci €8.50. Guided tours every Sat & Sun at noon, included in admission. The building next door to the Egyptian Museum houses the private art collection of aesthete and 1950s racing driver Francisco Godia. Harnessing medieval art, ceramics and modern Catalan art, in many ways it serves as a taster for the huge collections at Montjuïc in MNAC (see p.109), while its small size makes it immediately more accessible. In hushed rooms, where the only sound is the hum of the air conditioning, lie selected Romanesque carvings, Gothic altarpieces and *modernista* and *noucentista* paintings, combined with a varied selection of ceramics from most of the historically important production centres in Spain. Not all of the collection can be shown at any one time, so pieces are rotated on occasion, while special exhibitions also run in tandem, to which there's usually no extra charge.

La Pedrera

Pg. de Gràcia 92, entrance on c/Provença ☎ 902 400 973, ⊛ www.caixacatalunya.es/obrasocial. Daily 10am–8pm. €7. La Pedrera de Nit June–Aug only, Fri & Sat at 9.30pm, €11, advance sales from TelEntrada ☎ 902 101 212, ⊛ www.telentrada.com. Antoni Gaudí's weird apartment building at the top of Passeig de Gràcia is simply not to be missed – though you can expect queues whenever you visit. Built as the Casa Milà between 1905 and

1911 – but popularly known as La Pedrera, "the stone quarry" – its rippled facade, curving around the street corner in one smooth sweep, is said to have been inspired by the mountain of Montserrat, while the apartments themselves, whose balconies of tangled metal drip over the facade, resemble eroded cave dwellings. Indeed, there's not a straight line to be seen – hence the contemporary joke that the new tenants would only be able to keep snakes as pets. The self-guided visit includes a trip up to the extraordinary terrace to see at close quarters the enigmatic chimneys, as well as an informative exhibition about Gaudí's work displayed under the brick arches of the attic. "El Pis" on the building's fourth floor recreates the design and style of an early twentieth-century apartment. Perhaps the best experience of all is *La Pedrera de Nit*, when you can enjoy the rooftop and night-time cityscape with a complimentary *cava* and music – advance booking is essential.

La Pedrera is still split into private apartments and is administered by the Fundació Caixa de Catalunya. Through the grand main entrance of the building you can access the Fundació's first-floor **exhibition hall** (daily 10am–8pm; free; guided visits Mon–Fri at 6pm), which hosts temporary art shows of works by major international artists.

Vinçon

Entrances at Pg. de Gràcia 96, c/Provença 273 and c/Pau Claris 175 ☎932 156 050, ✆www.vincon.com. Mon–Sat 10am–2pm & 4.30–8.30pm. Right next to La Pedrera, the Vinçon store emerged in the 1960s as the country's pre-eminent purveyor of furniture and design. Pioneered by Fernando Amat, known as the "Spanish Terence Conran", the shop is filled to the brim with stylish and original household items. Apart from checking out the extraordinary furniture floor, which gives access to a terrace with views of La Pedrera, try and make time for *La Sala Vinçon* (open same hours as the store). This is Vinçon's exhibition hall and art gallery, which puts on shows of new design and furniture.

Palau Robert

Pg. de Gràcia 107 ☎932 384 000, ✆www.gencat.net/probert. Mon–Sat 10am–7pm, Sun 10am–2.30pm. Free. The information centre for the region of Catalunya hosts regularly changing exhibitions on all matters Catalan, from art to business. It's also an important concert venue for recitals and orchestras, while the pretty gardens around the back are a popular meeting point for the local nannies and their charges. The office inside is a handy place to pick up local touring and accommodation

▼ PALAU ROBERT

information, and there's a gift and bookshop in the former carriage courtyard that opens off Passeig de Gràcia.

Casa de les Punxes

Avgda. Diagonal 416–420. No public access. Architect Puig i Cadafalch's largest work, the soaring Casa Terrades, is more usually known as the Casa de les Punxes ("House of Spikes") because of its red-tiled turrets and steep gables. Built in 1903 for three sisters, and converted from three separate houses spreading around an entire corner of a block, the crenellated structure is almost northern European in style, reminiscent of a Gothic castle.

▲ CASA DE LES PUNXES

Casa Elizalde

C/de Valencia 302 ☎ 934 880 590. Mon–Fri 5–8pm, Sat & Sun 11am–2pm & 5–8pm. The Dreta's nicest intimate venue hosts regular exhibitions and film shows about *modernisme* and related themes. Classical concerts are also held here, usually with low-cost or free entry – check the posters at the entrance for details.

Mercat de la Concepció

Between c/de Valencia and c/d'Aragó ☎ 934 575 329, ⊛www.laconcepcio .com. Mon 8am–3pm, Tues–Fri 8am–8pm, Sat 8am–4pm; July & Aug closes at 3pm. The early fifteenth-

century Gothic church and cloister of La Concepció once stood in the old town, part of a convent abandoned in the early nineteenth century and then transferred here brick by brick in the 1870s. The adjacent market was built in 1888, its iron-and-glass tram-shed structure reminiscent of others in the city. Flowers and plants – a Concepció speciality – spill out of the entrance on c/de Valencia, and there are a couple of good snack bars just inside the market.

Shops

Antonio Miró

C/Consell de Cent 349 ☎ 934 870 670, ⊛www.antoniomiro.es; plus *Groc*, Rambla de Catalunya 100 ☎ 932 150 180. The showcase for Barcelona's most innovative designer, Antonio Miró, especially good for classy men's suits. There are Miró designs, shoes and denim for men and women, plus other labels, at the *Groc* outlet.

Armand Basi

Pg. de Gràcia 49 ☎ 932 151 421, ⊛www.armandbasi.com. Colourful men's and women's clothes, jackets and accessories from the hot Spanish designer.

BD Ediciones de Diseño

C/Mallorca 291 ☎ 934 586 909, ⊛www.bdlove.com. A design showroom at the cutting edge of Barcelona style. The building (Casa Thomas) is by Domènech i Montaner, the interior filled with the very latest in furniture and household design.

Bulevard Rosa

Pg. de Gràcia 55, entrances on Rambla Catalunya, c/de Valencia and c/d'Arago ☎ 933 090 650, ⊛www.bulevardrosa .com. Barcelona's first shopping arcade features over one hundred shops, specializing in chic designer gear, shoes and accessories.

Casa del Llibre

Pg. de Gràcia 62 ☎932 723 840, ⊛www.casadellibro.com. This is Barcelona's biggest book emporium, strong on literature, humanities and travel, with lots of English titles. There's a café at the back.

Colmado Quilez

Rambla de Catalunya 63 ☎932 152 356. A classic Catalan grocery, windows and shelves piled high with tins, preserves, bottles, jars and packets, plus a groaning *xarcuteria* counter.

Dom

C/de Provença 249 ☎934 871 181, ⊛www.id-dom.com. Original, amusing household and personal items (alarm clocks to olive-oil

▼ FLOWERS AT MERCAT DE LA CONCEPCIÓ

dispensers, knives and forks to bouncy chairs) at accessible prices.

Joaquín Berao

Rambla de Catalunya 74 ☎932 150 091, ⊛www.joaquinberao.com. Avant-garde jewellery by a Madrid designer in a beautifully presented shop.

Laie

C/Pau Claris 85 ☎933 181 739, ⊛www.laie.es. The Eixample's favourite bookshop, with an excellent selection of humanities and literature, and lots of English-language titles. Take a break in the upstairs café-restaurant (see p.130).

Mandarina Duck

Pg. de Gràcia 44 ☎932 720 364. Funky, colourful travel bags, backpacks, handbags and other carriers.

Mango

Pg. de Gràcia 8–10 ☎934 121 599 and Pg. de Gràcia 65 ☎932 157 530, plus others, ⊛www.mango.com. Now available worldwide, Barcelona is where high-street fashion chain *Mango* began (and prices here are cheaper than in North America and other European countries).

Muxart

C/Rosselló 230 ☎934 881 064, and Rambla de Catalunya 47 ☎934 677 423, ⊛www.muxart.com. Barcelona's top-class shoe designer, pricey gems for men and women.

Zara

Pg. de Gràcia 16 ☎933 187 675, Rambla de Catalunya 67 ☎932 160 868, plus others, ⊛www.zara.com. Trendy but cheap seasonal fashion from the Spanish chain, now with shops in over forty countries.

▲ HOTEL RITZ DOORMAN

Cafés

Forn de Sant Jaume

Rambla de Catalunya 50 ☎932 160 229. Mon–Sat 9am–9pm. Glittering windows piled high with goodies from this classic old *patisseria* and *bomboneria* – croissants, cakes and sweets, either to take away or eat at the adjacent café.

Laie Llibreria Café

C/Pau Claris 85 ☎933 027 310. Mon–Fri 9am–1am, Sat 10am–1am. Head up the stairs in front of the bookshop, either to the bar and mezzanine seating or the roomier salon at the back under bamboo matting. The buffet breakfast spread is popular, and there are set lunch and dinner deals, a la carte dining, and magazines to browse.

Valor

Rambla de Catalunya 46 ☎934 876 246. Mon–Thurs 8.30am–1pm & 3.30–11pm, Fri–Sun 9am–midnight. Ornate uptown chocolate specialist, serving the gentle folk since 1881. A warming hot choc and *xurros* (doughnut sticks) sends you happily on your way on a chilly morning.

Restaurants and tapas bars

ba-ba-reeba

Pg. de Gràcia 28 ☎933 014 302. Daily 7.30am–1.30am. A big range of tapas, from all corners of Spain, spreads along a twenty-metre bar in this slick, industrial-sized operation. It sees a lot of business- and shopping-traffic, and caters for all needs from breakfast to supper time and beyond.

Bodegueta

Rambla Catalunya 100 ☎932 154 894. Daily 8am–2am; closed mornings in Aug. Long-established basement *bodega* with *cava* by the glass, a serious range of other wines, and good ham, cheese, anchovies and other tapas to soak it all up.

Casa Calvet

C/de Casp 48 ☎934 124 012. Mon–Sat 1–3.30pm & 8.30–11.30pm. Dining in Gaudí's wonderfully decorated Casa Calvet is a glam night out. A seasonally changing, modern Catalan menu runs the gamut from simple (shrimp with home-made pasta and parmesan) to elaborate (duck livers with a balsamic vinegar reduction), and the desserts – some of which you have to order on arrival – are an artwork in themselves. From around €50 plus drinks; reservations advised.

Ciudad Condal

Rambla de Catalunya 18 ☎933 181 997. Daily 7.30am–1.30am. Breakfast sees the bar groan under the weight of a dozen types of crispy baguette sandwich, piled high on platters, supplemented by a cabinet of croissants and pastries, while the tapas selection ranges far and wide: *patatas bravas* to octopus.

East 47

Hotel Claris, c/Pau Claris 150 ☏934 874 647. Daily 1–4pm & 8–11.30pm. The hip hotel features an equally cutting-edge restaurant, serving creative Mediterranean cuisine under the gaze of a line of Warhol self-portraits. The beautifully presented dishes mix flavours with seeming abandon – like salad leaves with crispy bamboo, or coffee-scented cod – while the fearsomely fashionable staff work hard at making you feel at home. Expect to spend €70 and upwards. Reservations advised.

▲ UPTOWN SHOPPING MALL

Japonés

Ptge. de la Concepció 2 ☏934 872 592, ⊕www.grupotragaluz.com /japones. Mon–Thurs & Sun 1.30–4pm & 8.30pm–midnight, Fri & Sat 1.30–4pm & 8pm–1am. Designer style – gunmetal grey interior, staff-in-black service – at moderate prices gives this minimalist Japanese restaurant the edge over its more traditional rivals. Tick your choices from the long menu and hand it to the waiter; average meal cost is around €20–25 a head.

Muscleria

C/Mallorca 290 ☏934 589 844. Mon–Fri 1–4pm & 8.30pm–midnight, Sat 8.30pm–1am. Barcelona's mussels specialist, with a score of sauces/toppings on pots and platters, accompanied by some of the best fries in the city – for around €10 a serving. Sautéed clams, octopus or deep-fried squid are offered as starters, and there are a few salad-and-snack plates offered, but basically if bivalves don't appeal you're in the wrong place.

Mussol

C/Aragó 261 ☏934 876 151; branch at c/de Casp 19 ☏933 017 610. Meals daily 1pm–1am. Big rustic diners of the type that's all the rage in the city, known for their meat and vegetables *a la brasa*, most of which run between €5 and €10. *Calçots* (big spring onions) are a spring speciality, while snails (*cargols*) are on the menu all year round. It opens early for sandwich-and-croissant breakfasts for city workers.

O'Nabo de Lugo

C/de Pau Claris 169 ☏932 153 047. Mon–Sat 1–4pm & 8.30pm–midnight. A la carte meals in this renowned Galician seafood restaurant can easily top €50, but the budget-conscious can enjoy a three-course lunch for a mere €10 (even less if you eat in the bar), drink included. Thick, meaty broth usually figures, and simple standards like *botifarra* and potatoes – for more choice (and for some fish), trade up to the €16.50 *menú especial*.

Thai Gardens

C/Diputació 273 ☎934 879 898. Daily 1.30–4pm & 8.30–midnight, until 1am at weekends. Enjoy an excellent Thai set lunch (Mon–Fri only), or an all-out *menu degustació* for €30 – an English-language menu smooths the way, offering things like a creamy prawn and vegetable curry or fiery lamb strips cooked in Thai basil.

Tragaluz

Ptge. de la Concepció 5 ☎934 870 621, ⊛www.grupotragaluz.com /tragaluz. Daily 1.30–4pm & 8.30pm–midnight, until 1pm Thurs–Sat. Attracts beautiful people by the score, and the classy Mediterranean-with-knobs-on cooking, served under a glass roof (*tragaluz* means "skylight"), doesn't disappoint. Mains are from €18, though cheaper eats are served downstairs courtesy of the *Tragarapid* menu (dishes €6–8, served daily 1pm–midnight), where things like blinis, fajitas or a club sandwich cater for those fresh off the *modernista* trail (La Pedrera is just across the way).

Tramoia

Rambla de Catalunya 15 ☎934 123 634. Daily 7.30am–1.30am. Fashionable multi-space eatery for anything from a coffee and croissant to a filling meal. Snack downstairs on tapas and *torrades*, or head upstairs for Catalan brasserie food, including meat, fish and seasonal vegetables straight from the grill.

Bars

Cervesera Artesana

C/Sant Agustí 14 ☎932 379 594, ⊛www.lacervesera.net. Mon–Sat 6pm–1am. Catalan brew-pub serving a house IPA ("Iberian Pale Ale") and stout, plus a whole host of other speciality and bottled beers.

Les Gens Que J'aime

C/Valencia 286 ☎932 156 879. Daily 7pm–2.30am. It takes your eyes a while to adjust as you descend into the intimate *fin-de-siècle* interior of red velvet seats, dimmed lights and soulful mood music. As a refuge from the club scene, it's very pleasant for a relaxing drink.

Clubs

Mond Club

Sala Cibeles, c/Corsega 363 ☎932 720 910, ⊛www.mondclub.com. Fri 12.30–6am. Old ballroom converted into stylish Friday-night club, with a bit of everything thrown into the mix – punk, glam, electronica and guest DJs. The pre-club sister bar is *Mond Bar*, in nearby Gràcia (Pl. del Sol 21; daily 8.30pm–3am), where "pop will make us free".

▼ UPTOWN TAPAS BAR

Sagrada Família and Glòries

The easternmost reaches of the Eixample are dominated by the one building that is an essential stop on any visit to Barcelona – Antoni Gaudí's great church of the Sagrada Família. In many ways this has become a kind of symbol for the city, representing the glory of Catalan design and endeavour. Most visitors make a special journey out by metro to see the church and then head straight back into the centre, but it's worth diverting the few blocks south to the area known as Glòries for a further set of attractions, including the city's biggest flea market and Catalunya's flagship national theatre building.

Sagrada Família

C/Mallorca 401, entrance on c/de la Marina ☎932 073 031, ⊛www .sagradafamilia.org. Daily: April–Sept 9am–8pm; Oct–March 9am–6pm. €8, or €11 including guided tour. The overpowering church of the Sagrada Família ("Sacred Family") occupies an entire city block between c/de Mallorca and c/de Provença – the metro drops you right outside. Begun in 1882 on a modest scale, the 31-year-old architect Antoni Gaudí took charge of the project two years later and changed its scale immediately, seeing in the Sagrada Família an opportunity to reflect his own deepening spiritual feelings. He spent the rest of his life working on the church and was adapting the plans ceaselessly right up to his untimely death. Run over by a tram on June 7, 1926, his death was treated as a Catalan national disaster, and all of Barcelona turned out for his funeral procession.

By the time of Gaudí's death only one facade of the Sagrada Família was complete. Although the building survived the Civil War, Gaudí's plans and models were destroyed in 1936 by the anarchists, who regarded the church as a conservative religious relic. Work restarted in the late 1950s amid great controversy, with some maintaining that the

▼ SAGRADA FAMÍLIA

CAFÉS, TAPAS AND RESTAURANTS

Arco Iris	3
Bar Gaudí	2
Gorría	4
Piazzenza	1

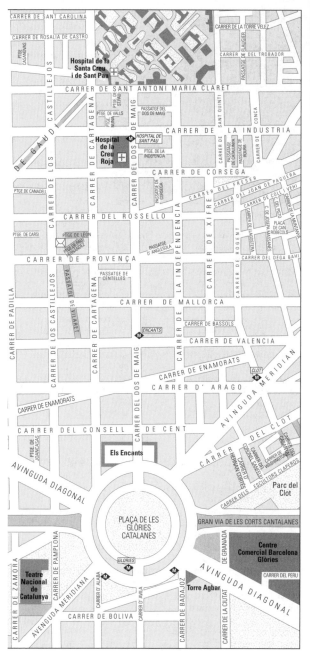

▲ MOSAIC DETAIL, HOSPITAL DE LA SANTÁ CREU I DE SANT PAU

Sagrada Família should be left incomplete as a memorial to Gaudí, others that the architect intended it to be the work of several generations. As the project draws inexorably towards realization (current projections predict a completion date of around 2017), a fresh set of arguments has arisen as to how to wrap the whole thing up – whether to continue with the original grandiose design or to go for a quicker but more modest alternative.

Gaudí's plan was to build a church capable of seating over 10,000 people. Eight spires – symbolic of the apostles – rise to over 100m: Gaudí planned to build four more and to add a 170-metre tower topped with a lamb (representing Jesus) over the transept. A precise symbolism also pervades the facades, each of which is divided into three porches devoted to faith, hope and charity. Gaudí made extensive use of human, plant and animal models in order to produce exactly the likenesses he sought for the building's sculptural groups.

In reality the place looks like a giant building site, but a recognizable church interior is starting to take shape, and if you take the **elevator** (€2) up one of the towers around the rose window, you'll be rewarded by partial views of the city through an extraordinary jumble of latticed stonework, ceramic decoration, carved buttresses and sculpture. There's also access to the crypt, where a small museum (opening times as for the church) traces Gaudí's career and the history of the church. Models, sketches and photographs help to make some sense of the continuing project, and you can view the sculptors and model-makers at work. The **guided tours** run hourly between April and October, reduced to four daily from Friday to Monday between November and March.

Hospital de la Santa Creu i de Sant Pau

C/de Sant Antoni Maria Claret 167 ☏ 934 882 078, ⊛ www.santpau.es. Tours in English/Spanish, Sat & Sun 10am–2pm, every 30min. €4.20.

Domènech i Montaner's innovative public hospital (1901–10) is possibly the one building that can touch the Sagrada Família for harmony, size and invention. Craftsmen adorned every inch with sculpture, mosaics, stained glass and ironwork, while much of the actual business of running a hospital was hidden away in underground corridors, which connect the buildings together. The *modernista* hospital buildings are now deemed to have served their purpose; behind them spreads the high-tech central block of the new hospital, due to be fully operational by 2006. The pavilions will then probably be turned over to educational or cultural use (a Museum of Medicine is mooted), though in the meantime there are guided tours of the complex, which can tell you more about the 600-year history of the hospital.

Casa Macaya

Pg. de Sant Joan 108. Just four blocks from the Sagrada Família, Josep Puig i Cadafalch's palatial Casa Macaya (1898–1900) is a superbly ornamental town house with a Gothic-inspired courtyard and canopied staircase from which griffins spring. It's rich in imaginative exterior carvings by craftsman Eusebi Arnau, who included an angel holding a camera and a tiny figure riding a bicycle among the more orthodox medieval symbols. The house is now in use as an exhibition space.

▼ ELS ENCANTS

Els Encants

C/Dos de Maig ☎ 932 463 030. Mon, Wed, Fri & Sat 9am–6pm; plus Dec 1–Jan 5 Sun 9am–3pm. An absolute must for flea-market addicts, the open-air Els Encants – properly the Mercat Fira de Bellcaire – takes up the entire block below c/Consell de Cent. You name it, you can buy it: old sewing machines, cheese graters, photograph albums, cutlery, lawnmowers, piles of clothes, shoes and CDs, antiques, furniture and out-and-out junk. Go in the morning to see it at its best. Haggling is de rigueur, but you're up against the experts.

Plaça de les Glòries Catalanes

Barcelona's major avenues all meet at the unkempt swirling traffic-circle-cum-park whose dedicatory plaques celebrate the Catalan "glories", from *modernisme* to Gothic architecture. The park itself (currently undergoing remodelling) is at the centre of the city's latest wave of regeneration. Towering above is Jean Nouvel's cigar-shaped **Torre Agbar**, a distinctive aluminium-and-glass tower inspired by the rocky protuberances of Montserrat. At 142m high, it's the third largest building in the city. **Avinguda Diagonal** shoots off to the southeast, with its new tram service running down to the Diagonal Mar district, while across Gran Via de les Corts Catalanes the play and park areas of **Parc del Clot** show what can be done in an urban setting within the remains of a razed factory site.

Teatre Nacional de Catalunya

Pl. de les Arts 1 ☏933 065 700, ⓦwww.tnc.es. Box office open Mon noon–3pm & 4–9pm, Tues–Sat noon–9pm, Sun noon–6pm. Catalunya's National Theatre was specifically conceived as a venue to promote Catalan productions, and features a repertory programme of translated classics (such as Shakespeare in Catalan), original works and productions by guest companies from elsewhere in Europe. The building itself makes a dramatic statement, designed by Ricardo Bofill and presenting the neighbourhood with a soaring glass box encased within a Greek temple on a raised dais, surrounded by manicured lawns. There are guided building and backstage **tours** for anyone interested in learning more (Tues, Wed & Fri at 10am, 11am & noon; €1.50; reservations required).

L'Auditori

C/Lepant 150 ☏932 479 300, ⓦwww.auditori.org. Box office open Mon–Sat noon–9pm, Sun 1hr before concert. The city's main contemporary concert hall, built in 1999, is home to the Orquestra Simfònica de Barcelona i Nacional de Catalunya (OBC), whose weekend concert season runs from September to May. Many other concerts take place here year-round, including chamber pieces, music for children and performances under the auspices of the annual autumn Contemporary Music Festival. It's also hoped that the city's music museum (currently closed) will be relocated here. Under-26s with ID get fifty percent discount on all tickets, an hour before the performance. The "Bus de les Arts" runs back to Plaça de Catalunya after concerts.

Plaza de Toros Monumental and Museo Taurino

Gran Via de les Corts Catalanes 749 ☏932 455 804. Museum: Mon–Sat 10.30am–2pm & 4–7pm, Sun 11am–1pm; €4. Bullfights: April–Sept, usually Sun at 7pm; €15–75. The city's only surviving working bullring provides a taste of Andalucia with its brick facade, Moorish egg-shaped domes, polychromatic decoration and *sol y sombra* ("sun and shade") seating sections. It's not a pastime with much of a following in Barcelona and, tellingly, the ring is one part of the city where not a word of

▼ TEATRE NACIONAL DE CATALUNYA

Catalan is seen. Bullfight costumes, posters, photographs and the stuffed heads of vanquished bulls occupy the small museum (enter at corner with c/de la Marina), while an overhead walkway outside the ring provides a view into the bull pens.

Shops

Centre Comercial Barcelona Glòries

Avgda. Diagonal 208, at Pl. de les Glòries Catalanes ☎ 934 860 404, ⓦ www.lesglories.com. Huge 230-store mall with all the national high-street fashion names (H&M, Zara, Bershka, Mango) as well as children's wear, toys and games, ice-cream parlours, a dozen bars, cafés and restaurants (open daily 10am–1am) and a seven-screen cinema complex.

Cafés

Bar Gaudí

Mercat de la Sagrada Família, c/de Padilla 255; no phone. Tues–Thurs 7am–2pm & 5.30–8.30pm, Fri 7am–8.30pm, Sat 7am–3pm. Only two blocks east of the Sagrada Família – and not a tourist in sight. The stand-up market bar has pastries, sandwiches and tapas at local prices, and an internal courtyard with a small children's playground.

Restaurants and tapas bars

Arco Iris

C/Roger de Flor 216 ☎ 934 582 283. Mon–Sat 1–4pm; closed Aug. Simple café serving a four-course lunchtime veggie *menú del dia* for around €9 (drinks extra). Typically, you'll start with a cream of vegetable soup or consommé, and finish with fresh fruit.

Gorría

C/de la Diputacio 421 ☎ 932 451 164, ⓦ www.restaurantegorria.com. Mon–Sat 1–3.30pm & 9–11.30pm; closed Aug. This elegant family-owned restaurant serves the finest seasonal Basque cuisine, like *pochas de Sanguesa* (a sort of white-bean stew), clams and hake in *salsa verde*, or wood-grilled lamb and suckling pig. Prices are on the high side (around €50 a head), but this is regional Spanish cooking of the highest order.

Piazzenza

Avgda. Gaudí 27–29 ☎ 934 363 817. Daily 1pm–1am; closed 2 weeks in Aug. A reliable standby just five minutes' walk from the Sagrada Família. There are tapas and drinks, and good-sized pizzas, served outdoors in summer, and you can eat for around €15.

Esquerra de l'Eixample

The long streets west of Rambla de Catalunya as far as Barcelona Sants train station – making up the Esquerra de l'Eixample – are perhaps the least visited on any city sightseeing trip. With all the major architectural highlights found on the Eixample's eastern (or right-hand) side, the Esquerra (left-hand side) was intended by its nineteenth-century planners for public buildings and institutions, many of which still stand. However, the Esquerra does have its moments of interest – not least in an eye-catching public park or two – while it's here that some of the city's best bars and clubs are found, particularly in the gay-friendly streets of the so-called Gaixample district, near the university.

Universitat de Barcelona

Gran Via de les Corts Catalanes 585, at Pl. de la Universitat ☏ 934 021 100, ⊛ www.ub.es. Built in the 1860s, the Neoclassical university building is now mainly used for ceremonies and administration purposes, but no one minds if you stroll through the main doors. There's usually an exhibition in the echoing main hall, while beyond lie two fine arcaded courtyards and extensive gardens.

▼ PARC DE L'ESPANYA INDUSTRIAL

Escola Industrial

Corner of c/del Comte d'Urgell and c/del Rossello. The Battló textile mill underwent major refurbishment in 1908 to emerge as the Escola Industrial. It occupies four entire Eixample blocks, with later academic buildings added in the 1920s, including a chapel by Joan Rubió i Bellvér, who worked with Antoni Gaudí. Students usually fill the courtyards, and you're free to take a stroll through to view the highly decorative buildings.

Museu i Centre d'Estudis de l'Esport

C/de Buenos Aires 56–58 ☏ 934 192 232. Mon–Fri 10am–2pm & 4–8pm. Free. Built as the Casa Companys in 1911 by Josep Puig i Cadafalch, the little cream-coloured house contains probably the most unassuming sporting "Hall of Fame" found anywhere in the world. In a couple of quiet, wood-panelled rooms photographs of 1920s Catalan rally drivers and footballers are

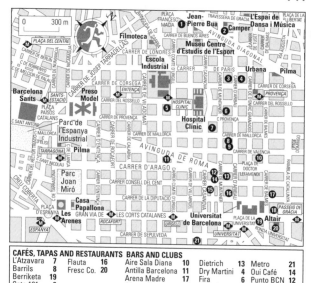

CAFÉS, TAPAS AND RESTAURANTS		BARS AND CLUBS					
L'Atzavara	7	Flauta	16	Aire Sala Diana	10	Dietrich	13	Metro	21
Barrils	8	Fresc Co.	20	Antilla Barcelona	11	Dry Martini	4	Oui Café	14
Berriketa	19			Arena Madre	17	Fira	6	Punto BCN	12
Cata 181	9			Airena Classic	17	La Boïte	1	Quilombo	3
Cubanito	15			Arena VIP	18	Luz de Gas	2	Sante Café	5

displayed alongside a varied collection of memorabilia, from a signed waterpolo ball used in the 1992 Olympics to Everest mountaineer Carles Vàlles' ice pick.

L'Espai de Dansa i Música

Trav. de Gràcia 63 ☎934 143 133. Box office open Mon–Sat 6.30–10pm, Sun 5–9pm. The "dance and music space" is the city's best bet for contemporary dance performances, bolstered by a varied programme of concerts by Catalan and other regional soloists and music groups.

Filmoteca

Avgda. de Sarrià 33 ☎934 107 590, ⊛http://cultura.gencat.es/filmo. Run by the Catalan government, the *Filmoteca* has an excellent cinema programme, showing three or four different films (often foreign, and usually in

their original language, marked "V.O.") every day. There's a children's club (*sessió infantil*) on Sunday, and a decent café attached to the cinema. Tickets are around €3, or you can buy a discounted pass allowing entry to ten films.

Parc de l'Espanya Industrial

C/de Sant Antoni. Daily 10am–dusk. Basque architect Luis Peña Ganchegui's urban park lies 2min walk around the southern side of Barcelona Sants station. Built on the site of an old textile factory, it has a line of red-and-yellow-striped concrete lighthouses at the top of glaring white steps with an incongruously classical Neptune in the water below. Altogether, six sculptors are represented here and, along with the boating lake, café kiosk, playground and sports facilities provided, the park takes a decent stab at reconciling local interests with the mundane nature of the surroundings.

Parc Joan Miró

C/de Tarragona. Daily 10am–dusk. Parc Joan Miró was laid out on the site of the nineteenth-century municipal slaughterhouse. It features a bare, raised piazza whose only feature is Joan Miró's gigantic mosaic sculpture *Dona i Ocell* ("Woman and Bird"), towering above a shallow reflecting pool. The rear of the park is given over to games areas and landscaped sections of palms and firs, with a kiosk café and some outdoor tables found in among the trees. The children's playground here is one of the best in the city, with a climbing frame and aerial runway as well as swings and slides.

Les Arenes

Pl. d'Espanya. The traditional bullring backing Parc Joan Miró is undergoing a massive Richard Rogers-inspired refit, to convert it into a leisure and retail complex with enormous roof terrace, while retaining the circular Moorish facade of 1900. To the side of the bullring, on c/de Llança, you can view one of the city's favourite house facades, namely the huge ceramic butterfly crowning the six-storey *modernista* **Casa Papallona** (1912).

Shops

Altair

Gran Via de les Corts Catalanes 616 ☏933 427 171, ✆www.altair.es. Travel books, guides, maps and world music, plus a programme of travel-related talks and exhibitions.

Camper

C/Muntaner 248 ☏932 013 188, and others, ✆www.camper.com. Spain's favourite shoe store opened its first shop in Barcelona in 1981. Providing hip, well-made, casual city footwear at a good price has been the cornerstone of its success.

Jean-Pierre Bua

Avgda. Diagonal 469 ☏934 397 100, ✆www.jeanpierrebua.com. The city's temple for fashion victims: a postmodern shrine for Yamamoto, Gaultier, Miyake, McCartney, Westwood, Miró and other international stars.

▼ BARCELONA SANTS TRAIN STATION

Pilma

Avgda. Diagonal 403 ☎934 161 399,
and c/de Valencia 1 ☎932 260 676,
ⓦwww.pilma.com. Inspiring venues
for stylish household furniture,
lighting, and kitchen and
bathroom goods and accessories.

Urbana

C/Còrsega 258 ☎932 187 036. The
place to browse for restored
mirrors, fireplaces and other
fittings rescued from
demolition.

Restaurants and tapas bars

L'Atzavara

C/Muntaner 109 ☎934 545 925.
Mon–Sat 1–4pm. Lunch-only spot
for fresh-tasting vegetarian
dining on proper tablecloths.
For €9 you choose from half a
dozen starters and soups, three
mains and four puds. Drinks are
another €1 on top – an all-
round bargain.

Barrils

C/d'Aribau 89 ☎934 531 091. Daily
9am–2am; closed Tues, and first two
weeks in July. Hanging hams and
barrels set the tone inside, and
the stuffed boar and moose keep
watch on punters tucking into
good, country-style tapas –
cured meats and Galician
seafood a speciality. Lunch is
around €8; otherwise, a la carte
meals cost €20–30. A sheltered
terrassa provides a breath of
summer air.

Berriketa

Gran Via de les Corts Catalanes 596
☎933 424 144. Daily 8am–1am.
Basque-run establishment with
reasonably priced tapas,

including *chistorra* (spicy sausage)
from Pamplona. *Txacolí* (Basque
white wine) is the stuff to drink
with it. There's a restaurant
(1–4pm & 8.30pm–midnight)
too, with grill-house specialities
and a €12 *menú del dia*.

Cata 181

C/de Valencia 181 ☎933 236 818.
Mon–Thurs 6pm–midnight, Fri & Sat
6pm–1am; closed Aug. The sleekest,
most respected of city wine bars
has a long wine list and an
accompanying menu of creative
tapas that many consider reason
enough to come in the first
place. It's a bit precious, but not
too expensive, with wines
(though not the best ones) from
€2 and most dishes around
€5–7.

Cubanito

C/Casanova 70 ☎934 543 188.
Tues–Fri 1–4.30pm & 8.30pm–1am,
Sat & Sun 8.30pm–1am; closed lunch
in Aug. Fresh and funky
Gaixample restaurant offering a
mix of Cuban and Catalan food
at moderate (€10–12) prices.
Home-style Cuban classics
include an appetizer of fried
green bananas, followed by *ropa
vieja* ("old clothes") – shredded
veal in tomato sauce.

Flauta

C/d'Aribau 23 ☎933 237 038.
Mon–Sat 8am–1am. Bar at the
front, dining room at the back,
this is a real local favourite for
the €9 lunchtime *menú del dia*,
which shows a bit more
adventure than many. It's also a
handy pit stop for a stuffed
flauta – a thin, crispy baguette
sandwich – or a range of tapas.

Fresc Co.

Ronda Universitat 29 ☎933 016 837, and others. Daily 1–5pm & 8pm–1am. Packed-out self-service diner with an enormous salad bar and selection of pizzas, pastas and desserts. No atmosphere, apart from the general hubbub at peak trough times, but you can pile your plate high for €7 at lunch (Mon–Fri) or €9 evenings and weekends.

Bars

Aire Sala Diana

C/de Valencia 236 ☎934 515 812. Thurs–Sat 11.30pm–3am, Sun 6–10pm. The hottest, most stylish lesbian bar in town is a surprisingly relaxed place for a drink and a dance to pop, house and retro sounds. Gay men are welcome too.

Dietrich

C/Consell de Cent 255 ☎934 517 707. Mon–Thurs 10pm–2.30am, Fri–Sun 10pm–3am. Cornerstone of the Gaixample scene is this fashionable late-night bar – *tranquilo* during the week, but ever more hedonistic as the weekend wears on.

Dry Martini

C/d'Aribau 166 ☎932 175 072. Mon–Thurs 1pm–2.30am, Fri & Sat 1pm–3am, Sun 6.30pm–2.30am. Legendary Barcelona cocktail bar, the rich dark wood and brass-highlighted interior exuding confident luxury. Business types dominate in the early evening, while a younger set moves in on weekend nights.

Fira

C/de Provença 171 ☎617 776 589. Tues–Thurs & Sun 11pm–3am, Fri & Sat 11pm–5am. One of the city's

most bizarre drinking emporiums comes complete with old-fashioned fairground rides and circus paraphernalia. Sit at the bar fashioned from a circus awning, or cosy up in the dodgem cars.

Oui Café

C/Consell de Cent 247 ☎934 514 570. Mon–Thurs & Sun 5pm–2am, Fri & Sat 5pm–3am. A gay meet-and-greet destination, with a popular summer *terrassa*.

▲ DIETRICH BAR

Punto BCN

C/Muntaner 63–65 ☎934 536 123. Daily 6pm–2.30am. Gaixample classic that attracts a lively crowd for drinks, chat and music. Wednesday happy hour is a blast, while Friday night is party night.

Quilombo

C/d'Aribau 149 ☎934 395 406. Mon–Thurs & Sun 9pm–3am, Fri & Sat 7.30pm–3.30am. Unpretentious music bar that's rolled with the years (since 1971), featuring live guitarists, South American bands and a clientele that joins in enthusiastically.

Sante Café

C/d'Urgell 171 ☎933 237 832. Mon–Fri 8am–3pm, Sat & Sun 5pm–3am; closed Aug. A minimalist sort of place that's more of a café during the day, but chills out at night, with DJs guesting at the weekend.

Clubs

Antilla Barcelona

C/Aragó 141–143 ☎934 514 564, ⊛www.antillasalsa.com. Daily 10.30pm–5am, weekends until 6am. Caribbean tunes galore: rumba, son, salsa, merengue, mambo – you name it. There are live bands, killer cocktails, and dance classes most nights.

Arena Madre

C/Balmes 32 ☎934 878 342, ⊛www.arenadisco.com. The "mother" club (Tues–Sat 12.30–5am, Sun 7pm–5am) sits at the helm of *Arena*'s gay empire, all within a city block, which includes the high-disco antics of *Arena Classic* (c/de la Diputació 233; Fri & Sat 12.30–5am) and more of the same plus house and garage at the more mixed *Arena VIP*

(Grand Via de les Corts Catalanes 593; Fri & Sat 12.30–6am).

La Boite

Avgda. Diagonal 477 ☎933 191 789, ⊛www.masimas.com. Regular jazz and blues sessions, plus funk, soul and salsa, with gigs on Monday to Saturday from around midnight. Tickets cost from €9, rising to €22 for big names.

Luz de Gas

C/Muntaner 246 ☎932 097 711, ⊛www.luzdegas.com. Smart venue popular with a slightly older crowd, playing live music (local rock, blues, soul, jazz and covers) every night around midnight. Foreign acts appear regularly too, mainly jazz-blues types but also old soul acts and up-and-coming rockers.

Metro

C/Sepúlveda 158 ☎933 235 227, ⊛www.metrodiscobcn.com. Mon–Thurs & Sun midnight–5am, Fri & Sat midnight–6am. A gay institution in Barcelona, with cabaret nights and other events midweek, and extremely crowded club nights at weekends in its two rooms playing either current dance and techno or retro disco.

Gràcia and Parc Güell

Gràcia was a village for much of its early existence, before being annexed as a suburb of the city in the late nineteenth century. It's traditionally been a stronghold of the liberal intelligentsia, though Gràcia also has a genuine local population that still lends it an attractive small-town atmosphere. Consequently, its annual summer festival, the Festa Major every August, has no neighbourhood peer. Much of the pleasure here is serendipitous – wandering the narrow, gridded streets, catching a film or otherwise, taking time out from the rigours of city-centre life. However, no one should miss the opportunity to visit nearby Parc Güell, an extraordinary flight of fancy by architectural genius Antoni Gaudí. To get to Gràcia take the FGC train from Plaça de Catalunya to Gràcia station, or the metro to either Diagonal, to the south, or Fontana, to the north. From any of the stations, it's around a 500-metre walk to Gràcia's main square, Plaça del Sol, hub of the neighbourhood's renowned nightlife.

Mercat de la Llibertat

Pl. de la Llibertat ☎ 932 170 995. Mon 8am–3pm, Tues–Thurs 8am–2pm & 5–8pm, Fri 7am–8pm, Sat 7am–3pm; closed afternoons in Aug. Many of Gràcia's locals start every morning the same way – shopping for bread and provisions, and grabbing a quick coffee, in the busy neighbourhood market. The building was revamped in 1893 by Francesc Berenguer i Mestrès, a former pupil of Gaudí, who sheltered its food stalls and kiosks under a *modernista* wrought-iron roof.

Casa Vicens

C/de les Carolines 24. No public access. Antoni Gaudí's first major private commission (1883–85) took inspiration from the Moorish style, covering the facade of the house in linear green-and-white tiles with a flower motif. The decorative iron railings are a reminder of Gaudí's early training as a metalsmith, and to further prove his versatility – and demonstrate how Art Nouveau cuts across art forms – Gaudí designed much of the mansion's original furniture, too.

▼ SNAILS AT THE MERCAT DE LA LIBERTAT

CAFES, TAPAS AND RESTAURANTS

Café del Sol	9
Flash, Flash	15
Glop	7
Habibi	16
Illa de Gràcia	11
Miria	12
Mos	1
Nou Candanchu	14
Octubre	10
Roble	13

BARS AND CLUBS

Canigó	8
Casa Quimet	3
Centre Artesà Tradicionàrius	5
Otto Zutz	2
Salambo	6
Virreina	4

Plaça de la Virreina

This pretty square, backed by the much-restored parish church of Sant Joan, is one of Gràcia's favourites, with the *Virreina Bar* (see p.151) and others providing a place to rest and admire the handsome houses, most notably Casa Rubinat (1909), at c/de l'Or 44, the last major work of Francesc Berenguer. Children and dogs, meanwhile, scamper around the small drinking fountain.

Plaça de Rius i Taulet

The thirty-metre-high clock tower in the heart of Gràcia was a rallying point for nineteenth-century radicals – whose twenty-first-century counterparts prefer to meet for brunch at the square's popular café *terrassas*.

Parc Güell

C/d'Olot. Daily: March & Oct 10am–7pm; April & Sept 10am–8pm; May–Aug 10am–9pm; Nov–Feb 10am–6pm. Free. Gaudí's Parc Güell (1900–14) was his most ambitious project after the Sagrada Família, conceived as a "garden city", of the type popular at the time in England. In the end, only two houses were actually built, and the park was officially opened to the public instead in 1922. Laid out on a hill, which provides fabulous views back across the city, the park is an almost hallucinatory expression of the imagination. Pavilions of contorted stone, giant decorative lizards, meandering rustic viaducts, a vast Hall of Columns, carved stone trees – all combine in one manic swirl of ideas and excesses. Perhaps the most famous element is the long, meandering ceramic bench that snakes along the edge of the terrace above the columned hall. The displays at

▲ CHILLIDA SCULPTURE, PARC DE LA CREUETA DEL COLL

the **Centre d'Interpretació** (daily 11am–3pm; €2), at the main park entrance, provide useful background information on the whole project.

It's best to visit Parc Güell during the week if you can, as weekends can be very busy. The most direct route there is on bus #24 from Plaça de Catalunya, Passeig de Gràcia or c/Gran de Gràcia, which drops you at the eastern side gate by the car park. From Metro Vallcarca, walk a few hundred metres down Avinguda de l'Hospital Militar until you see the mechanical escalators on your left, ascending Baixada de la Glòria – follow these to the western side park entrance (15min in total). From Metro Lesseps, turn right along Travessera de Dalt and then left up steep c/Larrard, which leads (10min) straight to the park's main entrance on c/Olot. There's a small café in the park, and several others along c/Larrard.

Casa Museu Gaudí

Parc Güell ☎ 932 193 811. Daily: April–Sept 10am–8pm; Oct–March 10am–6pm. €4. One of Gaudí's collaborators, Francesc Berenguer, designed and built a turreted house within Parc Güell for the architect (though he only lived in it intermittently). This now contains a diverting collection of some of the furniture Gaudí designed for other projects – a typical mixture of wild originality and brilliant engineering – as well as plans and objects related to the park and to Gaudí's life.

Parc de la Creueta del Coll

Pg. de la Mare de Deu del Coll 89. Daily 10am–dusk. Parc de la Creueta del Coll was laid out around a small artificial lake on the site of an old quarry. There's a stand of palm trees, a café kiosk, and concrete promenades under the sheer quarry walls, but it's all been allowed to go to the dogs (and feral cats) a bit lately and could do with a spruce-up. Still, you're greeted at the top of the park steps by an Ellsworth Kelly metal spike, while suspended by steel cables over a water-filled quarry corner is a massive concrete claw by the Basque artist Eduardo Chillida. Bus #28 from Plaça de Catalunya, up Passeig de Gràcia, stops just 100m from the park steps, or you can walk up Passeig de la Mare de Deu del Coll from Metro Vallcarca in about twenty minutes (there's a neighbourhood map at the metro station).

Shops

Camisería Pons

C/Gran de Gràcia 49 ☎ 932 177 292.

Modernista shirt shop transformed into a showcase for Spanish fashion designers.

Contribucions

C/Riera de Sant Miquel 30 ☎932 187 140. Gràcia's well-known discount outlet for Spanish and Italian designer labels.

Cafés

Café del Sol

Pl. del Sol 16 ☎934 155 663. Daily 1pm–2.30am. This hugely popular neighbourhood café-bar sees action day and night. The seats outside provide a window onto the local comings and goings; otherwise you can drink in the bar until late.

Mos

Via Augusta 112 ☎932 371 313. Daily 7am–10pm. Self-service, designer style – browse the sleek counters under the suspended ceiling, pick up a croissant or tuna turnover, or maybe one of the cooked dishes, pasta servings or seasonal salads, and finish off with a handmade chocolate, a house speciality.

▼ CAFÉ DEL SOL

Restaurants and tapas bars

Flash, Flash

C/de la Granada del Penedès 25 ☎932 370 990. Daily 1pm–1.30am, bar open 11am–2am. Tortillas (most around €5) served any way you like, from plain and simple to elaborately stuffed, with sweet ones for dessert. If that doesn't grab you, there's a small menu of salads, soups and burgers. Either way, you'll love the white leatherette booths and monotone cutouts – very Austin Powers.

Glop

C/Sant Lluís 24 ☎932 137 058. Tues–Sun 1–4pm & 8pm–1am. The rusticity (stone-flagged floors, baskets of garlic) stops just the right side of parody and the lunch *menú del dia* is one of the city's best deals; otherwise expect to spend around €15 a head for grills and other tavern specials prepared in front of you on the open kitchen ranges. At the weekend you may have to wait for a table.

Habibi

C/Gran de Gràcia 7 ☎932 179 545. Mon–Fri 1pm–1am, Sat 2–4.30pm & 8pm–1am. Bright and breezy North African dining room, with a summer *terrassa*. The Plat Habibi gives you a taste of all the house specials – from a minty *tabbouleh* to chicken *schawarma*. Add a fresh-squeezed juice (there's no alcohol served), home-made dessert and a mint tea, and you're still unlikely to spend more than €12.

Illa de Gràcia

C/Sant Domènec 19 ☎932 380 229. Tues–Fri 1–4pm & 9pm–midnight, Sat

▲ FLASH, FLASH RESTAURANT

& Sun 2pm–midnight; closed mid-Aug to mid-Sept. Decorative harmony reigns in this spacious, sleek vegetarian dining room, where the food is a cut above – think grilled tofu, stuffed aubergine gratin or wholewheat spaghetti carbonara.

Miria

Pl. Rius i Taulet 11 ⊕ 932 185 198. Daily 1–4pm & 7–11pm. The sunny *terrassa* on the square is half the attraction, but it's nice inside, too – simple but stylish, with mellow sounds to accompany the well-priced food. A la carte favourites include great soups, pastas with a choice of sauces and designer salads, while there's a bargain weekend *menú del dia* that provides three sample-starters, main course and dessert for around €10 (drinks extra).

Nou Candanchu

Pl. Rius i Taulet 9 ⊕ 932 377 362. Mon, Wed, Thurs & Sun 7am–1am, Fri & Sat until 3am. Sit beneath the clock tower in summer and choose from the wide selection of dishes – tapas and hot sandwiches, but also steak and eggs, steamed clams and mussels, or cod and hake cooked plenty of different ways. It's managed by an affable bunch of young guys, and there's lots of choice for €6–11.

Octubre

C/Julian Romea 18 ⊕ 932 182 518. Mon–Fri 1.30–3.30pm & 9–11pm, Sat 9–11pm; closed Aug. For romance and the food to go with it, it's hard to beat this warm, rustic little charmer. The Catalan menus are seasonal and somewhat unpredictable, but constants are the sensational desserts and the hard-to-beat prices – usually around €20 for three sparkling courses. Reservations advised.

Roble

C/Luis Antunez 7 ⊕ 932 187 387. Mon–Sat 7am–midnight. The neighbourhood's choicest tapas selection, with food served promptly either at the bar or at one of the wooden tables. Nudge your way up to the counter and peruse the day's specials, or browse the list on the wall.

Bars

Canigó

Pl. de la Revolució 10; no phone.
Tues–Sun 11am–midnight. Family-
run neighbourhood bar now
entering its third generation. It's
not much to look at, but it's a
friendly spot, packed out at
weekends with a young, hip and
largely local crowd meeting to
chew the fat.

Casa Quimet

Rambla del Prat 9 ☏932 175 327.
Tues–Sun 6.30pm–2am; closed Aug.
At the "guitar bar" you have to
supply the music yourself: pick
out your favourite from the
collection and try your luck.
The place is crammed with old
photographs and trinkets.

▲ VIRREINA BAR

Salambo

C/Torrijos 51 ☏932 186 966. Daily
noon–2.30am. Stylish
neighbourhood drink-and-meet
spot. The pre- and post-cinema
crowd pops in for *cafetières* of
coffee, sandwiches and meals,
and there are lots of wines and
cava by the glass. Upstairs, you
can shoot pool.

Virreina Bar

Pl. de la Virreina 1 ☏932 379 880.
Mon–Thurs & Sun 10am–1pm, Fri &
Sat 10am–2am. Popular local bar
with seats outside in one of
Gràcia's loveliest squares. A great
place to enjoy hard-to-find
Trappist beers from Belgium.

Clubs

Centre Artesà Tradicionàrius

Trav. de Sant Antoni 6–8 ☏932 184
485, ◎www.tradicionarius.com. Folk
recitals by Catalan and visiting
performers, usually on Friday
around 10pm (tickets €8) –
though the bar is open nightly.
Also sponsors an annual
international folk and traditional
dance festival between January
and April, with performances
here and at other city venues.

Otto Zutz

C/de Lincoln 15 ☏932 380 722,
◎www.grupo-ottozutz.com. Tues–Sat
midnight–6am. Still one of the
most fashionable places in the
city, this three-storey former
textile factory has a dance floor,
three bars, VIP lounge and a
shedload of pretensions. With
the right clothes and face, you're
in (you may or may not have to
pay, depending on how
impressive you are, the day of
the week, etc).

Camp Nou, Pedralbes and Sarrià-Sant Gervasi

On the northwestern edge of the city centre, the city's famous football stadium, Camp Nou, draws locals and visitors alike, both to the big game and to the FC Barcelona museum. The nearby suburb of Pedralbes, across Avinguda Diagonal, contains two interesting museums (of decorative art and ceramics), while a half-day's excursion can be made of the trip by walking from the museums, past an early Gaudí creation, to the calm cloister and celebrated art collection at the Gothic monastery of Pedralbes. You can complete the day by returning via Sarrià, just to the east, more like a small town than a suburb, with a pretty main street and market to explore. At night, the focus shifts southeast to neighbouring Sant Gervasi and the style bars in the streets north of Avinguda Diagonal.

Camp Nou and FC Barcelona

Avgda. Arístides Maillol ☎934 963 600, ⌨www.fcbarcelona.com. Match tickets (€30–60) also from ServiCaixa ☎902 332 211, ⌨www.servicaixa.com. m Collblanc/Maria Cristina. In Barcelona, football is a genuine obsession, with support for the local giants FC (Futbol Club) Barcelona raised to an art form. The magnificent Camp Nou football stadium was built in 1957, and enlarged for the 1982 World Cup semi-final to accommodate 98,000 spectators. Although the club was among the most successful in Spain in the 1990s, its fortunes have waned recently in favour of Valencia and, particularly, of arch rival Real Madrid. However, it's always been more than just a football club to the locals, and during the Franco years the club stood as a Catalan symbol, around which people could rally.

The football season runs from late August until May, with games usually played on Sundays (though sometimes on other days). You'll have little problem getting a match ticket, except perhaps for the biggest domestic games and major European ties. For all other games, some tickets are put on general sale a week before each match, or try calling ServiCaixa. Touts at the ground also offer tickets for most matches.

The stadium complex also boasts a museum (see opposite) and hosts basketball games with FC Barcelona's professional team, while there's also a public ice rink, stadium souvenir shop and café.

Museu del Futbol

Camp Nou, Avgda. Arístides Maillol ☏934 963 600, ⊛www.fcbarcelona .com. Mon–Sat 10am–6.30pm, Sun 10am–2pm. €5, guided tours €9. The museum at the Barcelona football stadium is a splendid celebration of Spain's national sport. There's an excellent English-language photo-history, an audiovisual display of goals galore, and team and match photos dating back to 1901, including a gallery of the celebrated foreign players who have graced Barça's books: as early as 1911, there were five British players in the team. The tour, meanwhile, includes a visit to the glittering trophy room and a view of the stunning tiered seating and pitch.

Palau Reial de Pedralbes

Avgda. Diagonal 686. m Palau Reial. The Palau Reial de Pedralbes – basically a large villa with pretensions – was built for the use of the royal family on their visits to Barcelona, with the funds raised by public subscription. It received its first such visit in 1926, but within five years the king had abdicated and the palace somewhat lost its role. Franco kept it on as a presidential residence and it later passed to the city, which since 1990 has used its rooms to show off its fine ceramics and decorative arts collections in two separate museums: the Museu de Ceràmica, and the Museu de les Arts Decoratives (see below). The gardens (free entry) are a calm oasis.

Museu de Ceràmica

Avgda. Diagonal 686 ☏932 801 621, ⊛www.museuceramica.bcn.es. Tues–Sat 10am–6pm, Sun 10am–3pm. €3.50, free on first Sun of the month; ticket also valid for Museu de les Arts Decoratives and Museu Tèxtil i d'Indumentària in La Ribera. The bulk of the exhibits range from the thirteenth to the nineteenth centuries, and include splendid Moorish-influenced tiles and plates from the Aragonese town of Teruel, as well as a series of fifteenth- and sixteenth-century *socarrats* – decorated terracotta panels – from Paterno displaying demons and erotic scenes. Perhaps the most vivid examples of the work coming out of Barcelona and Lleida workshops of the time are the two extensive *azulejo* (tile) panels of

▼ PALAU REIAL DE PEDRALBES

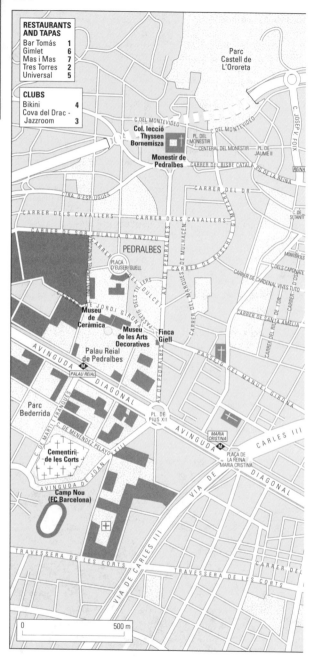

RESTAURANTS AND TAPAS

Bar Tomás	1
Gimlet	6
Mas i Mas	7
Tres Torres	2
Universal	5

CLUBS

Bikini	4
Cova del Drac - Jazzroom	3

Parc Castell de L'Ororeta

C. DEL MONTEVIDEO

C. DEL MONTEVIDEO

PL. DEL MONESTIR

C. JOSEP V. FOIX

Col·lecció Thyssen Bornemisza

CENTRAL DEL MONESTIR

PL. DE JAUME II

REINA

Monestir de Pedralbes

CARRER DEL BISBE CATALÀ

FC DE LA REINA

CARRER DEL DR

C. DE SETANTI

CTRA. D'ESPLUGUES

CARRER DELS CAVALLERS

CARRER DELS CAVALLERS

MONTEVOLS

C.DELS CAPONATE

CARRER DE SOR EULALIA D'ANZIZU

PEDRALBES

CARRER DE CARDENAL VIVES TUTO

PLAÇA D'EUSEBI GUELL

PASSEIG DELS TIL·LERS

CARRER DE MULHACÉN

CARRER DEL MARQUÈS DE BRAGA

CARRER DE SANTA AMELIA

AV. DE PEDRALBES

AV. DE JORDI GIRONA

PASSEIG DELS TIL·LERS DULCET

Museu de Ceràmica

Museu de les Arts Decoratives

Finca Güell

AVINGUDA

DIAGONAL

Palau Reial de Pedralbes

PALAU REIAL

PASSEIG DEL MANUEL GIRONA

Parc Bederrida

PL. DE PIUS XII

C. DE MARTI I FRANQUES

C. DE MENENDEZ PELAYO

AVINGUDA

AVINGUDA

CARLES III

DIAGONAL

MARIA CRISTINA

PLAÇA DE LA REINA MARIA CRISTINA

Cementiri de les Corts

AVINGUDA DE JOAN XXIII

Camp Nou (FC Barcelona)

VIA DE CARLES III

VIA DE

DIAGONAL

TRAVESSERA DE LES CORTS

TRAVESSERA DE LES CORTS

CARRER DE

0	500 m

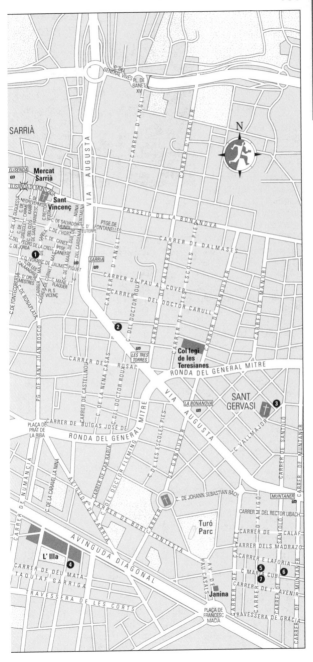

1710: one showing a Madrid bullfight, the other the feasting and dancing taking place at a party centred on the craze of the period – hot-chocolate-drinking.

Museu de les Arts Decoratives

Avgda. Diagonal 686
☎932 805 024, ⊛www
.museuartsdecoratives
.bcn.es. Tues–Sat 10am–
6pm, Sun 10am–3pm. €3.50, free on first Sun of the month; ticket also valid for Museu de Ceràmica and Museu Textil i d'Indumentària in La Ribera.
Arranged around the upper gallery of the Palau Reial's former throne room, the Decorative Arts Museum provides a fair old romp from Romanesque art through to contemporary Catalan design. Side rooms showcase the various periods under the spotlight, with displays of highly polished Baroque and Neoclassical furniture contrasting with the varied Art Deco and *modernista* holdings. The latter half of the gallery concentrates on Catalan *disseny* (design), from chairs to espresso machines, lighting to sink taps.

Finca Güell

Avgda. de Pedralbes 77. m Palau Reial.
Built as stables and a riding school for the family of Antoni Gaudí's patron, Eusebi Güell, the architect completed the *finca* in 1887, at the same time as he was working on the Palau Güell in the old town. The brick and tile buildings are frothy, whimsical affairs with more than a Moorish element to them and you are allowed no further than the gateway – but what a gateway. An extraordinary

▲ MUSEU DE LES ARTS DECORATIVES

winged dragon of twisted iron snarls at the passers-by, its razor-toothed jaws spread wide in a fearsome roar.

Monestir de Pedralbes

Bxda del Monestir ☎932 039 282, ⊛www.museuhistoria.bcn.es.
Tues–Sun 10am–2pm. €4, combination ticket with Col.lecció Thyssen-Bornemisza €5.50, free on first Sun of the month. m Palau Reial and 20min walk, or 30min ride on bus #22 from Plaça de Catalunya/Passeig de Gràcia or #64 Ronda Sant Antoni and c/d'Aribau. Founded in 1326 for the nuns of the Order of St Clare (whose members still reside here), this is in effect an entire monastic village preserved on the outskirts of the city, set within medieval walls and gateways that shut out completely the noise and clamour of the twenty-first century.

It took the medieval craftsmen a little over a year to prepare Pedralbes (from the Latin *petras albas*, "white stones") for its first community of nuns. The speed of the initial construction, and the subsequent uninterrupted habitation by the Order, helps explain the monastery's architectural harmony. The cloisters in particular are perhaps the finest in the city, built on three levels and adorned by the slenderest of columns. All around the cloisters are alcoves and rooms displaying the monastery's treasures – frescoes, paintings, memorabilia and religious artefacts – while the adjacent church retains some of its original fourteenth-century stained glass and the superb carved marble tomb of the foundation's sponsor, Elisenda de Montcada, wife of Jaume II, who died in 1364.

▲ GATEWAY, FINCA GÜELL

Col.lecció Thyssen-Bornemisza

Monestir de Pedralbes, Bxda del Monestir ☎ 934 811 041, ⊛ www.museothyssen.org. Tues–Sun 10am–2pm. €3.50, combination ticket with Monestir de Pedralbes €5.50, free on first Sun of the month. A small but superb art collection, covering five major movements in European art from the fourteenth to the eighteenth centuries, is on permanent view in one of the monastery's capacious old dormitories. The displays begin with a series of medieval Italian religious paintings, mostly of Madonna and Child, of which the undoubted highlight is the sublime *Madonna of Humility* by Fra Angelico, painted in 1433. The mainly Italian collection is offset by a group of works from the Flemish and German schools, most important of which are the dark, sombre depictions of saints by Cranach the Elder, which stand in sharp contrast to the exuberance of the Italian works of the same period. St George, a popular subject for Catalans, whose patron saint he is, is presented here as the all-conquering hero – albeit standing over the puniest dragon imaginable.

Parc Castell de l'Oreneta

C/Montevideo 45. Daily 10am–dusk. Bus #66 from Pl. Catalunya or #64 from Pl. Universitat. In the rural park on the slopes of the Collserola hills, behind Pedralbes monastery, there are miniature train rides and pony rides for children on Sundays.

Sarrià

FGC Sarrià c/Mare de Deu de Núria exit, or bus #64 from Pl. Universitat or Pedralbes. Sarrià's narrow traffic-free main street – c/Major de Sarrià – shows aspects of the independent small town that Sarrià once was. At its northern end, at Plaça de Sarrià, the much-restored church of Sant Vincenç flanks the main Passeig de la Reina Elisenda de Montcada, across which lies the neighbourhood market, **Mercat Sarrià** (Mon & Tues 8am–2.30pm, Wed & Thurs 8am–2.30pm & 5–8pm, Fri 8am–8.30pm, Sat 8am–3.30pm; July & Aug closes 2.30pm & closed Sat), housed in a *modernista* red-brick building of 1911. Carrer Major de Sarrià runs downhill from here, past other surviving old-town squares, prettiest of which is **Plaça Sant Vicenç** (off c/Mañe i Flaquer), where there's a statue of the saint and a nice little sandwich café-bar, the *Can Pau* (closed weekends). You also must not miss the *Bar Tomás* (see below), just around the corner on c/Major de Sarrià, for the world's best *patatas bravas*.

Avinguda Diagonal

The uptown section of Avinguda Diagonal runs through the heart of Barcelona's flashest business and shopping district. Typical of the enterprises here is L'Illa, the giant shopping centre (see opposite), whose 340-metre-long facade flanks the avenue – the stepped design is a prone echo of New York's Rockefeller Center. Smaller designer fashion stores are ubiquitous,

▼ PEDRALBES CHURCH

particularly around **Plaça Francesc Macià** and Avinguda Pau Casals – at the end of the latter, **Turó Parc** (daily 10am–dusk) is a good place to rest weary feet, with a small lake and a café-kiosk.

Shops

L'Illa

Avgda. Diagonal 555–559 ☏934 440 000, ⊚www.lilla.com. The landmark uptown shopping mall, stuffed full of designer fashion, plus FNAC (music and books), Sfera (cosmetics), Decathlon (sports), El Corte Inglés (department store), Caprabo (supermarket) and much more. You can get here on the **Tomb Bus shopping line service** from Plaça de Catalunya, which visits other uptown stores as well (daily every 7min; €1.25 each way, or €5 for one day's unlimited travel).

Janina

Avgda. Pau Casals 8 ☏932 020 693. Barcelona's premier lingerie designer, with own-label lingerie, swim- and sleepwear, plus items by other designers.

Restaurants and tapas bars

Bar Tomás

C/Major de Sarrià 49 ☏932 031 077. Daily except Wed 8am–10pm. The house *patatas bravas* – spicy fried potatoes with garlic mayo and *salsa picante* – is not all they serve in this utterly unassuming, white-Formica-table bar (the *croquetas* and *tuna empandillas* are great too), but it might as well be, as that's what the queues are for. They fry between noon and 3pm and 6pm and closing, so if it's *bravas* you want, note the hours.

Bars

Gimlet

C/Santaló 46 ☏ 932 015 306. Daily 7.30pm–2.30am. Especially popular in summertime, when the tables outside are packed with the local beautiful people, who come here for snacks and drinks.

Mas i Mas

C/Marià Cubì 199 ☏ 932 094 502, ⓦ www.masimas.com. Mon–Thurs & Sun 7pm–2.30am, Fri & Sat 7pm–3am. Cornerstone of the uptown bar scene and, in their own words, "a cross between a cocktail bar and a dancehall". The music policy is blues, acid-jazz, hip-hop and house, and the crowd young and funky.

Tres Torres

Via Augusta 300 ☏ 932 051 608. Mon–Sat 7pm–3am. Large *terrassa*-bar set in the beautiful grounds of an old house, which gets very crowded in summer.

Universal

C/Marià Cubì 182 ☏ 932 013 596. Mon–Sat 11pm–4.30am. A classic designer bar that's been at the cutting edge of Barcelona style since 1985. Be warned: they operate a strict door policy here, and if your face doesn't fit you won't get in.

Clubs

Bikini

C/Deu i Mata 105 ☏ 933 220 005, ⓦ www.bikinibcn.com. Tues–Sat midnight–5am. Not only regular rock gigs, but a night of clubbing variety – *Rock Room* for pop, rock and dance, Latin fusion in *Arutanga* and laid-back cocktail hour sounds in *Dry Bikini*.

Cova del Drac – Jazzroom

C/Vallmajor 33 ☏ 933 191 789, ⓦ www.masimas.com. Closed Mon, Sun & Aug. One of Barcelona's best jazz clubs serves up live music from 11pm, with a DJ to follow. Cover charge is €9–20 depending on the act.

Tibidabo and Parc del Collserola

The views from the heights of Tibidabo (550m), the peak that signals the northwestern boundary of the city, are legendary. On a clear day you can see across to Montserrat and the Pyrenees, and out to sea even as far as Mallorca. However, while many make the tram and funicular ride up to Tibidabo's amusement park and church, few realise that beyond stretches the Parc de Collserola, an area of peaks and wooded valleys roughly 17km by 18km, threaded by rivers, roads and hiking paths – one of Barcelona's best-kept secrets. You could walk into the park from Tibidabo, but it's actually better to start from the park's information centre, across to the east, above Vallvidrera, where hiking-trail leaflets are available.

Parc d'Atraccions

Pl. del Tibidabo ☏ 932 117 942, ⊛ www.tibidabo.es. Mid-June to mid-Sept daily noon–10pm, until 11pm at weekends; mid-Sept to mid-June Sat & Sun only noon–6pm. All rides €22, restricted rides €11, plus family/discount tickets. The Funicular del Tibidabo (see box) drops you right outside the gates of a wonderful amusement park, laid out around several levels of the mountaintop, connected by landscaped paths and gardens. It's a mix of traditional rides and high-tech attractions, many of which take full advantage of the park's location to offer jaw-dropping perspectives over the city. For a

Getting to Tibidabo

Reaching the heights of Tibidabo is half the fun, since you'll need to combine several forms of transport. First, take the FGC train (line 7) from Plaça de Catalunya station to Avinguda Tibidabo (the last stop). Emerging from the station escalators, cross the road to the tram/bus shelter at the bottom of the tree-lined avenue. The **Tramvia Blau**, an antique tram service (mid-June to mid-Sept daily 10am–8pm; rest of year weekends & hols 10am–6pm; departures every 15–30min; €2 one-way, €2.90 return) then runs you up the hill to Plaça Doctor Andreu; there's a bus service instead out of season during the week. Here, you change to the **Funicular del Tibidabo**, which has regular connections to Tibidabo at the top (operates when the Parc d'Atraccions is open; €2 one-way, €3 return). If the funicular isn't running, take a taxi from Avinguda Tibidabo instead, which will cost about €8 to Tibidabo. Alternatively, the special **Tibibus** runs direct to Tibidabo from Plaça de Catalunya, outside El Corte Inglés (weekends & hols year round every 30min; plus weekdays in summer hourly; €2). For details of public transport, call ☏ 010 or check out ⊛ www.tmb.net.

▲ VALLVIDRERA FUNICULAR

with a noisy *correfoc*, a theatrical fireworks display.

Sagrat Cor

Elevator operates daily 10am–2pm & 3–7pm. €1.50. Next to Tibidabo's amusement park, climb the shining steps of the Templo Expiatorio de España – otherwise known as the Sagrat Cor (Sacred Heart) – to the dramatic, wide balcony for some stunning views. The church is topped with a huge statue of Christ and, inside the church, a lift (*ascensor*) takes you higher still, to just under the statue's feet, from where the city, surrounding hills and sea shimmer in the distance.

Torre de Collserola

Carretera de Vallvidrera al Tibidabo ☎934 069 354, ⓦwww .torredecollserola.com. Wed–Sun 11am–2.30pm & 3.30–7pm, July–Sept until 8pm. €5. Follow the road from the Tibidabo car park and it's only a few minutes' walk to

real thrill, try the aeroplane ride, a Barcelona icon; the red plane has been spinning since 1928. And don't miss the Museu d'Autòmates, a collection of coin-operated antique fairground machines in working order. Summer weekends end

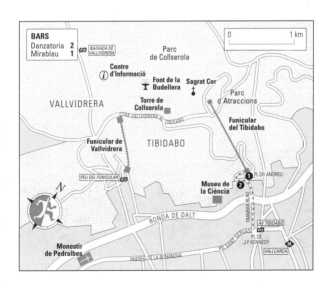

Norman Foster's soaring communications tower. High above the tree line, this features a glass lift that whisks you up ten floors (115m) for extensive views – 70km, they claim, on a good day.

Parc del Collserola

Centre d'Informació ☎ 932 803 552, ⓦhttp://ParcCollserola.amb.es. Daily 10am–3pm. FGC Baixada de Vallvidrera (on the Sabadell or Terrassa line from Pl. de Catalunya; 15min). The park information centre lies in oak and pinewoods, an easy ten-minute walk up through the trees from the FGC Baixada de Vallvidrera train station. There's a bar-restaurant here with an outdoor terrace, plus an exhibition on the park's history, flora and fauna, while the staff hand out English-language leaflets detailing the various park walks. Some of the well-marked paths – like the oak-forest walk – soon gain height for marvellous views over the tree canopy, while others descend through the valley bottoms to springs and shaded picnic areas. Perhaps the nicest short walk from the information centre is to the Font de la Budellera (1hr return), a landscaped spring deep in the woods. If you follow the signs instead from the *font* to the Torre de Collserola (another 20min), you can return to Barcelona on the funicular from the nearby suburban village of Vallvidrera (daily 6am–midnight; every 6–10min), which connects to Peu del Funicular, an FGC train station on the line from Plaça de Catalunya.

Museu de la Ciència

C/Teodor Roviralta 47–51 ☎ 903 223 040 or 932 126 050, ⓦwww .nuevomuseodelaciencia.com. Tues–Sun 10am–8pm. ADmission charged. The city's Science Museum has undergone massive refurbishment It was previously housed in a converted *modernista* hospice, and the new works have retained the original building but surrounded it by a park and added four times as much exhibition space in a huge underground extension. You can expect a fully interactive experience, touching on all aspects of science and tracing the history of matter from the origins of the universe onwards. Special exhibitions, talks and experiments are featured, and the popular planetarium from the original museum has been revived.

▲ MUSEU DE LA CIÈNCIA

▲ MIRABLAU BAR

Bars

Danzatoria

Avgda. Tibidabo 61 ☏ 932 116 261, ⊛ www.danzatoria.com. Wed–Sun 11pm–3am. Make the trip for the aerial views and drinks in a former mansion, set high above the city. There are four rooms and music styles, ten bars and – best of all – a fantastic garden, which makes this very pleasant for summer nights.

Mirablau

Pl. del Dr Andrea, Avgda. Tibidabo ☏ 934 185 879. Daily 11am–5am. Unbelievable city views from a chic bar near the Tibidabo funicular that fills to bursting at times.

Montserrat

The mountain of Montserrat, with its weirdly shaped rock crags, vast monastery and hermitage caves, stands just 40km northwest of Barcelona. It's the most popular day-trip from the city, reached in around ninety minutes by train and then cable car or rack railway for a thrilling ride up to the monastery. Once there, you can visit the basilica and monastery buildings and complete your day with a walk around the woods and crags, using the two funicular railways that depart from the monastery complex.

Aeri de Montserrat

Montserrat Aeri ☎932 051 515, ⓦwww.fgc.net. Departures every 15min, daily 9.25am–1.45pm & 2.20–6.45pm. €12 return from Barcelona. For the cable-car service, get off the train from Barcelona at Montserrat Aeri station (52min). You may have to wait in line fifteen minutes or so, but then it's only a five-minute swoop up the sheer mountainside to a terrace just below the monastery – probably the most exhilarating ride in Catalunya. Returning to Barcelona, the line R5 trains depart hourly from Montserrat Aeri (from 9.37am).

Cremallera de Montserrat

Monistrol de Montserrat ☎902 312 020, ⓦwww.cremalleramontserrat .com. Departures every 20min–1hr, daily 7.22am–6.38/8.38pm (most frequent, and later, services at

▲ AERI DE MONTSERRAT

Getting to Montserrat

To reach the Montserrat cable-car/rack-railway stations, take the **FGC train** (line R5, direction Manresa), which leaves daily from **Plaça d'Espanya** (ⓜ Espanya) at hourly intervals from 8.36am. You can buy through-transport tickets at Plaça d'Espanya (€12 return), while two combination tickets are also available: the **Transmontserrat** (€21), which includes all transport services, including unlimited use of the mountain funiculars; and the **Totmontserrat** (€34.50), which includes the same, plus monastery museum entry and a cafeteria lunch. **Bus tours** from the city (around €40; ask at any tourist office) also run to the monastery, but these can't compete for thrills with the do-it-yourself train and aerial rides.

weekends March–Oct, plus July–Sept).
€12 return from Barcelona. The
alternative approach to the
monastery is by the Montserrat
rack railway, which departs from
Monistrol de Montserrat station
(the next stop after Montserrat
Aeri, another 4min), and takes
twenty minutes to climb to the
monastery, via Monistrol-Vila.
The original rack railway on
Montserrat ran between 1892
and 1957, and this modern
replacement recreates the
majestic engineering that allows
the train to climb 550m in 4km.
Returning to Barcelona, the line
R5 trains depart hourly from
Monistrol de Montserrat (from
9.33am).

Monestir de Montserrat

Information office ☎938 777 701,
ⓦwww.abadiamontserrat.net. Daily
9am–5.45pm, July–Sept until 7pm.
Walking maps and accommodation
advice available. Legends hang
easily upon the monastery of
Montserrat. Fifty years after the
birth of Christ, St Peter is said
to have deposited an image of
the Virgin (known as La
Moreneta), carved by St Luke, in
one of the mountain caves. The
icon was lost in the early eighth
century after being hidden
during the Moorish invasion,
but reappeared in 880,
accompanied by the customary
visions and celestial music. A
chapel was built to house it, and
in 976 this was superseded by a
Benedictine monastery, set at an
altitude of nearly 1000m.
Miracles abounded and the
Virgin of Montserrat soon
became the chief cult-image of
Catalunya and a pilgrimage
centre second in Spain only to
Santiago de Compostela – the
main pilgrimages to Montserrat
take place on April 27 and

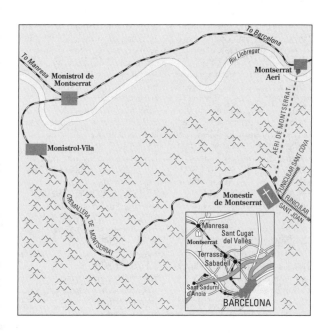

▲ MONESTIR DE MONTSERRAT

September 8. The monastery's various buildings – including hotel, post office, souvenir shop, bar, patisserie and supermarket – fan out around an open square, and there are extraordinary mountain views from the terrace as well as from various other vantage points scattered around the complex. There are plenty of places to eat, but all are relatively pricey and none particularly inspiring. Best views are from the *Restaurant de Montserrat*, in the cliff-edge building near the car park – the self-service cafeteria, one floor up, is where you eat with the all-inclusive *Tot Montserrat* ticket.

Basílica

Daily 8–10.30am & noon–6.30pm. Free. Of the religious buildings, only the Renaissance basilica, dating largely from 1560 to 1592, is open to the public. **La Moreneta**, blackened by the smoke of countless candles, stands above the high altar – reached from behind, by way of an entrance to the right of the basilica's main entrance. The approach to this beautiful icon reveals the enormous wealth of the monastery, as you queue along a corridor leading through the back of the basilica's rich side chapels. Signs at head height command "SILENCE" in various languages, but nothing quietens the line which waits to kiss the image's hands and feet.

The best time to be here is at the chanting of Ave Maria, daily at 1pm (noon on Sunday), when Montserrat's world-famous **boys' choir** sings. The boys belong to the Escolania, a choral school established in the thirteenth century and unchanged in musical style since its foundation.

Museu de Montserrat

Mon–Fri 10am–6.45pm, Sat & Sun 9.30am–7.45pm. €5.50. Near the entrance to the basilica, the monastery museum presents a few archeological finds brought back by travelling monks, together with painting and sculpture dating from the thirteenth century, including works by Caravaggio, El Greco, Tiepolo, Picasso, Dalí, Monet and Degas. Religious items are in surprisingly short supply, as most of the monastery's valuables were carried off by Napoleon's troops, who sacked the complex in 1811. The ticket also gets you in the **Espai Audiovisual** (daily 9am–6pm), near the information office, which tells you something of the life of a Benedictine community.

Mountain walks

Funicular departures every 20min, daily 10am–6pm, weekends only Oct–March. Santa Cova €2.50 return, Sant Joan €6.10 return, combination ticket €6.90. Following the mountain tracks to the caves and hermitages, you can contemplate what Goethe wrote in 1816: "Nowhere but in his own Montserrat will a man find happiness and peace." The going is pretty good on all the tracks and the signposting is clear, but you do need to remember that you are on a mountain. Take water if you're hiking far and keep away from the edges. Two separate funiculars run from points close to the cable-car station. One drops to the path for **Santa Cova**, a

seventeenth-century chapel built where the Moreneta icon is said originally to have been found. It's an easy walk of less than an hour there and back. The other funicular rises steeply to the hermitage of **Sant Joan**, from where it's a tougher 45 minutes' walk to the **Sant Jeroni** hermitage, and another 15 minutes to the Sant Jeroni summit at 1236m. Several other walks are also possible from the Sant Joan funicular, perhaps the nicest being the circuit around the ridge that leads in 45 minutes all the way back down to the monastery.

PLACES Montserrat

▼ CAKES AND HONEY STALL

Sitges

The seaside town of Sitges, 36km south of Barcelona, is definitely the highlight of the local coast – the great weekend escape for young Barcelonans, who have created a resort very much in their own image. It's also a noted gay holiday destination, with an outrageous annual Carnival (Feb/March) and a summer nightlife to match. During the heat of the day, though, the tempo drops as everyone hits the beach, while out of season Sitges is delightful: far less crowded, and with a temperate climate that encourages promenade strolls and old-town exploration.

The beaches

There are clean sands either side of the old town headland, though these become extremely crowded in high season. For more space it's best to keep walking west from Passeig de la Ribera along the palm-lined promenade of Passeig Marítim, past a series of eight interlinked beaches that runs a couple of kilometres down the coast as far as the *Hotel Terramar*. There are breakwaters, beach bars, restaurants, showers and watersports facilities along the way, with the more notorious

▲ BEACH AT SITGES

gay nudist beaches found at the far end – for these, keep on past *L'Atlantida* disco to the *Sun Beach Garden* beach bar (10min) and the small coves beyond.

Sitges information

Trains to Sitges (€2.25 each way) leave Passeig de Gràcia or Barcelona Sants stations every twenty minutes, more frequently at peak times (destination Vilanova/St Vicenç), and it's a thirty- to forty-minute ride depending on the service.

The town's **Oficina Turisme** (c/Sinia Morera 1, at Oasis shopping centre ☎938 945 004, ⊛www.sitges.com; July–Sept daily 9am–9pm; Oct–June Mon–Fri 9am–2pm & 4–6.30pm) is five minutes' walk from the train station. From here you can pick up useful restaurant and accommodation lists, and there's bike rental from **Sitges Bike** (☎938 949 458, ⊛www.sitgesbike.com; from €16 a day), located around the corner in Shop (Local) 34 of the Oasis shopping centre.

A **combination ticket** (€5.40, valid one month) is available for all three museums – note that **Monday** isn't the best day to come, as the museums and many restaurants are closed.

CAFÉS, TAPAS & RESTAURANTS
Al Fresco	4
Beach House	7
Celler Vell	1
Chiringuito	9
Fragata	10
Izarra	6
Pinta	8

BARS
Parrot's Pub	3
Vikingos	2
Voramar	5

Església Parroquial

Pl. del Baluard ☎938 940 374. Church usually open for Mass. The knoll overlooking the town beaches and marina is topped by the landmark Baroque parish church dedicated to Sant Bartolomeu, whose annual festival is celebrated in town in the last week of August. The views from the terrace sweep up and down the coast, while behind in the narrow streets of the old town you'll find a series of old whitewashed mansions, as well as the town hall and the brick Mercat Vell (Old Market), the latter now an exhibition hall.

Museu Cau Ferrat

C/Fonollar ☎938 940 364. July & Aug Tues–Sun 10am–2pm & 5–9pm; Sept–June Tues–Fri 10am–1.30pm & 3–6.30pm, Sat 10am–7pm, Sun 10am–3pm. €3. Artists were drawn to the town in the late nineteenth century by its light and views, and Sitges flourished as an important *modernista* centre under the patronage of artist and writer Santiago Rusiñol (1861–1931). His former house and workshop contains a massive jumble of his own paintings, as well as sculpture, painted tiles, drawings and various collected odds and ends – like the decorative ironwork Rusiñol brought back

▲ ESGLÉSIA PARROQUIAL

in bulk from the Pyrenees. The museum also contains works by the artist's friends (including Picasso), who used to meet both in Sitges and in Barcelona's *Quatre Gats* tavern.

Palau and Museu Maricel

C/Fonollar ☎938 940 364. Museum open July & Aug Tues–Sun 10am–2pm & 5–9pm; Sept–June Tues–Fri 10am–1.30pm & 3–6.30pm, Sat 10am–7pm, Sun 10am–3pm. €3. The museum in this lovely mansion near the church contains minor art works, medieval to modern, and maintains an impressive collection of Catalan ceramics and sculpture. In summer (usually two evenings a week), the main part of the mansion itself is open for guided tours, a short classical music concert and drinks – ask at the tourist office for the current schedule.

Museu Romàntic

C/Sant Gaudenci 1 ☎938 942 969. July & Aug Tues–Sun 10am–2pm & 5–9pm; Sept–June Tues–Fri 10am–1.30pm & 3–6.30pm, Sat 10am–7pm, Sun 10am–3pm. €3, access by guided tour only every hour. Occupying the stately rooms of Can Llopis, a bourgeois house of 1793, the so-called "Romantic Museum" aims to show the lifestyle of a rich Sitges family in the nineteenth century by displaying a wealth of period furniture and possessions, from divans to dolls.

Mercat Municipal

Avgda. Artur Carbonell ☎938 940 466. Mon–Thurs 8am–2pm, Fri & Sat 8am–2pm & 5.30–8.30pm. The town market is a great place to put together a beach picnic. Stalls offer cooked and cured meats, marinaded olives, cheese, anchovies, fresh bread, home - made crisps and fruit.

Shops

CyD

C/Major 60. Men's designer shirts in limited-edition styles – classic whites to vibrant colours.

Oscar

Pl. de l'Industria 2. Closed Mon. Swim, beach and clubwear for the very well-toned man about town.

Taller Antic

C/Fonollar. A treasure trove of Art Nouveau jewellery and nineteenth-century design pieces, from perfume bottles and picture frames to ornamental clocks and letter-openers.

Cafés

Al Fresco

C/Major 33 ☎938 113 307. Tues–Sun 9am–midnight. A crisp, white space open for breakfast, home-made cakes and light meals. The associated restaurant of the same name around the corner (c/Pau Barrabeitg 4; ☎938 940 600) serves fancier Catalan fusion meals, with mains (chargrilled tuna, lamb tagine, oven-baked monkfish) for around €15–20.

▲ SITGES MANSION

Chiringuito

Pg. de la Ribera ☎938 947 596. Daily 10am–10pm, reduced hours in winter. Claims to be Spain's oldest beach bar, serving grilled sardines, fried baby squid and calamari, sandwiches and snacks at budget prices on the prom.

Restaurants and tapas bars

Beach House

C/Sant Pau 34 ☎938 949 029, ⊛www.beachhousesitges.com. Easter–Nov only, daily 9am–2am. The Australian chef-owners have created a highly relaxed restaurant, with a *table d'hôte* menu (€20) that changes every couple of days and offers four courses of the best in Asian–Med fusion food. Breakfast and gourmet sandwiches are available until 4pm, an open-air terrace adds a touch of seaside romance, while "after-beach" happy hour cocktails are served daily (4–8pm).

Celler Vell

C/Sant Buenaventura 21 ☎938 111 961. Mon 1–4pm & 8–11pm, Tues 1–4pm, Thurs–Sun 1–4pm & 8–11pm. Traditional Catalan food in rustic surroundings, offering everything from grilled rabbit to sautéed beans with calamari. There's a good-value *menú del dia*, while dinner will cost between €20 and €30.

Fragata

Pg. de la Ribera 1 ☎938 941 086. Daily 1–4pm & 8–11pm. Typical of the new wave of classy seafood places in town, serving inventive fish, shellfish, rice and *fideuà* (noodle) dishes at moderate to expensive prices. Catch-of-the-day choices like monkfish casserole, *xató* (salt cod and anchovy salad) or grilled local prawns cost from €13 to €18.

Izarra

C/Major 22 ☎938 947 370. Daily 1.30–4pm & 8.30–11pm. Pint-sized Basque bar with a wide range of tapas and main meals. Cosy up to the bar, grab a plate and tuck in from the dishes arranged on the counter.

Pinta

Pg. de la Ribera 58–59 ☎938 947 871. Daily 1–4pm & 8pm–midnight. The enormous menu here concentrates on fish and seafood at affordable prices. The lunchtime *menú del dia* (not available weekends) is a bargain

€10, though a full meal including drinks can be had for around €30. The promenade-view terrace fills quickly at lunchtime.

Bars

Parrot's Pub

Pl. de l'Industria ☎ 938 947 881. Daily 6pm–2am. The stalwart of the gay bar scene in Sitges. Take a seat under the plastic raffia parasols and watch the parade, or check with the locals on the current club scene.

Vikingos

C/Marqués de Montroig 7–9 ☎ 938 949 687, ⊛ www.losvikingos.com. Mon–Thurs & Sun 11am–1am, Fri & Sat 11am–2am. Long-standing party-zone bar with an enormous air-conditioned interior and streetside terrace. Drinks, snacks or full meals served from morning to night.

Voramar

C/Port Alegre 55 ☎ 938 944 404. Daily 6pm–2am. This charismatic seafront bar features a few choice pavement tables and a panelled and carved interior that has the feel of an English pub. A mixed crowd of drinkers sinks ice-cold beers or the wicked house cocktails.

▼ PARROT'S PUB

Accommodation

Hotels

Finding a vacancy in a good hotel in Barcelona can be very difficult, and you're advised to book well in advance between Easter and the end of October. Prices are relatively high, too. The absolute cheapest double rooms in a simple family-run pension, sharing an outside shower, cost around €35, though €40–50 a night is more realistic. For air conditioning, a TV and an elevator to your room there's a fair amount of choice around the €60–90 mark, while up to €150 gets you the run of decent hotels in most city areas. For Barcelona's most fashionable hotels, count on €250–400 a night.

Prices given below are for the cheapest available double/twin room in high season, including the seven percent **tax** (IVA) that is added to all accommodation bills. Some places offer discounts in winter (Nov, Jan & Feb), or for longer stays, while the larger hotels often have special rates in August (when business travel is scarce) or at weekends.

Breakfast isn't usually included (even in very expensive places), unless specifically stated in the reviews. **Credit cards** are accepted almost everywhere, even in very modest places (though American Express isn't always). There's a lot of street noise in Barcelona, so bring earplugs if you're at all concerned.

On the Ramblas

Benidorm Ramblas 37 ☎933 022 054. Refurbished rooms opposite Plaça Reial that offer real value for money, hence the tribes of young tourists. Rooms available for one to five people, all with bathtubs and showers, and a Ramblas view if you're lucky (and prepared to pay a bit more). From €45.

Reservation agencies

You can book accommodation at the tourist offices (Turisme de Barcelona, see below), but only in person on the day or online – they do not have an advance telephone reservation service. Alternatively, contact one of the **reservation agencies** listed below. As well as finding hotels, some specialize in **apartment rentals** (starting at around €70–100 a night for a studio sleeping two), but make sure you understand all the costs – seasonal premiums, cleaning charges, utility bills and taxes can all push up the headline figure.

Barcelona Apartment Rentals UK ☎0117/907 3486, ☎www.barcelonaapartmentrentals.co.uk. A small range of quality apartments, mainly in the Eixample (some near the Sagrada Família) and Gràcia.

Barcelona On-Line Barcelona ☎902 887 017 or 933 437 993, ☎www.barcelona-on-line.es. Commission-free reservations for hotels, pensions and apartments.

My Favourite Things Barcelona ☎933 295 351 or 637 265 405, ☎www.myft.net. Has an eye for unusual and offbeat accommodation, from boutique hotels to private bed and breakfasts.

Turisme de Barcelona Offices in Barcelona at Pl. de Catalunya; Pl. de Sant Jaume; Barcelona Sants; Barcelona Airport ☎807 117 222, from abroad ☎932 853 1833, ☎www.barcelonaturisme.com. Same-day, commission-free accommodation bookings, in person, by phone, or on the website.

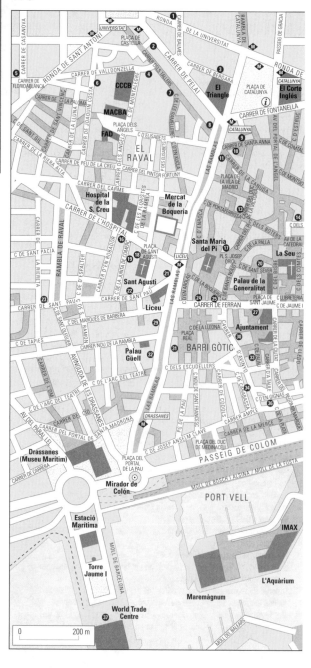

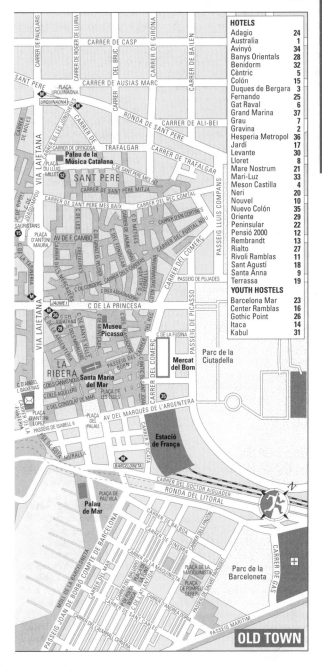

HOTELS

Adagio	24
Australia	1
Avinyó	34
Banys Orientals	28
Benidorm	32
Cèntric	5
Colón	15
Duques de Bergara	3
Fernando	25
Gat Raval	6
Grand Marina	37
Grau	7
Gravina	2
Hesperia Metropol	36
Jardí	17
Levante	30
Lloret	8
Mare Nostrum	21
Mari-Luz	33
Meson Castilla	4
Neri	20
Nouvel	10
Nuevo Colón	35
Oriente	29
Peninsular	22
Pensió 2000	12
Rembrandt	13
Rialto	27
Rivoli Ramblas	11
Sant Agustí	18
Santa Anna	9
Terrassa	19

YOUTH HOSTELS

Barcelona Mar	23
Center Ramblas	16
Gothic Point	26
Itaca	14
Kabul	31

OLD TOWN

Lloret Ramblas 125 ☏933 173 366, ☏933 019 283. Gilt mirrors, old paintings and wrinkled leather sofas in the lounge speak of a faded glory, and rooms are on the elderly side too, though bathrooms and tile floors have been upgraded. But it's a fine building in a good location, and many rooms have Ramblas-facing balconies – as does the dining room, where breakfast is available (not included). €80.

Mare Nostrum Ramblas 67 ☏933 185 340, ☏934 123 069. Comfortable double or triple/family rooms with satellite TV and air conditioning – nothing flashy, but modern, well kept and double-glazed against the noise. Some come with balconies and street views, others are internal. Breakfast included. €65, €75 en suite.

Oriente Ramblas 45 ☏933 022 558, ⊚www.husa.es. If you're looking for somewhere traditional on the Ramblas, this historic three-star is your best bet – mid-nineteenth-century style in the grand public rooms and tastefully updated bedrooms. Breakfast included. From €150.

Rivoli Ramblas Ramblas 128 ☏934 817 676, ⊚www.rivolihotels.com. The elegant, soundproofed rooms come with satellite TV and spacious bathrooms, the front ones with classic Ramblas views. There's also a lovely rooftop terrace and bar, while guests can also use the rooftop deck and small pool at the cheaper sister hotel, the *Ambassador*, across the Ramblas in the Raval. From €250.

Barri Gòtic

Adagio c/de Ferran 21 ☏933 189 061, ⊚www.adagiohotel.com. Rooms on five floors (there's an elevator) have been given a thorough refurbishment – new beds, parquet floors, satellite TV, air conditioning, soundproofing and decent bathrooms – and a buffet breakfast is included. Front and side rooms have little balconies. €90.

Avinyó c/d'Avinyó 42 ☏933 187 945, ⊚www.hostalavinyo.com. All the rooms here are freshly painted or tiled, with and without private bath, and all boast a ceiling fan. There's a fair amount of space and some rooms have little sofas. Note that c/d'Avinyó is noisy at weekends. No credit cards. €40, en suite €55.

Colón Avgda. Catedral 7 ☏933 011 404, ⊚www.hotelcolon.es. Splendidly situated four-star hotel, opposite the cathedral – rooms at the front throw open their windows to balconies with superb views. It's an old-money kind of place, with faithful-retainer staff and huge public salons. "Superior" rooms have an Edwardian lounge area and highly floral decor, though other rooms are more contemporary. From €250.

Fernando c/de Ferran 31 ☏933 017 993. Rooms at these prices fill quickly; that they're also light, modern and well kept by friendly people is a real bonus. All come with sinks and TV, with or without attached shower. Dorm accommodation (€19) is available on the top floor in rooms that sleep four to eight, some with attached bathroom. €40, en suite €50.

Hesperia Metropol c/Ample 31 ☏933 105 100, ⊚www.hesperia-metropol.com. Stylish conversion of an older building that – because it's slightly off the beaten old-town track – has remarkably good prices. The lobby is a masterpiece of contemporary design, while rooms are understated but comfortable – street noise isn't too bad, either. From €120.

Jardí Pl. Sant Josep Oriol 1 ☏933 015 900, ⊚hoteljardi@retemail.es. The location sells this place – overlooking the charming Plaça del Pi – which explains the steepish prices for rooms that, though smart and modern, can be a bit bare and even poky. But the bathrooms have been nicely done, and some rooms (the top ones have terraces) look directly onto the square. You can have breakfast here (not included), but the *Bar del Pi* in the square is a better bet. €80.

Levante Bxda. Sant Miquel 2 ☏933 179 565, ⊚www.hostallevante.com. A backpackers' favourite with fifty rooms – singles, doubles, twins, triples – on two rambling floors. Some rooms are much better than others (with newer pine furniture, en-suite bathrooms and balconies), while the comings and goings aren't to everyone's liking, but prices are reasonable. €50, en suite €60.

Mari-Luz c/de la Palau 4, 2° ☏ & ☏933 173 463, ⊚pensionmariluz@menta.net.

This old mansion, on a quieter than usual Barri Gòtic street, has six inexpensive doubles with shared bathrooms. Someone's been to IKEA for furniture and there are art prints on the walls, laundry facilities and a small kitchen. The drawback is that this is a hostel, too, with 35 dorm beds (€15–18 depending on season) in various other rooms, and it's a tight squeeze when full. From €40.

Neri c/de Sant Sever 5 933 040 655, ⊛www.hotelneri.com. Eighteenth-century palace close to the cathedral that's given the boutique treatment to its 22 stylish rooms and filled them the latest mod cons – plasma-screen TV, movies on demand, Internet access and CD player. A tranquil roof terrace provides a nice escape, and there's a good contemporary Mediterranean restaurant attached. From €180.

Nouvel c/Santa Anna 18–20 ☎933 018 274, ⊛www.hotelnouvel.com. Rooms differ in size at this 1920s era hotel, but come with brass or wooden bedsteads, high ceilings, air conditioning and compact bathrooms – one has a jacuzzi bath. It's best at the back, where rooms have little sunny terraces, though four spacious corner rooms at the front have curvaceous double balconies. Be warned – the street might be pedestrianized, but it's not noise-free. Breakfast included. €120.

Rembrandt c/Portaferrissa 23 ☎ & ☎933 181 011. Standard rooms have a balcony or little patio, while larger ones are more versatile – one has a gallery (with single bed above the double) and large corner bath, while a rather Victorian-looking "suite" (two rooms split by hanging net curtain) can sleep two or four. The friendly owners will also serve you breakfast, sell you a beer, or rent you a fan. From €50, gallery €60, suite €75/90.

Rialto c/de Ferran 42 ☎933 185 212, ⊛www.gargallo-hotels.com/rialto. A three-star hotel that's more like a family-run concern, with carpeted corridors and heavy doors leading into updated period rooms with parquet flooring, oak furniture and country-style furnishings. There's a good buffet breakfast. €100.

Santa Anna c/Santa Anna 23 ☎933 012 246. Attractive little rooms on two floors,

many with a small balcony onto the street or the rear. Room 202 has a lovely private terrace, though the bathroom for this one is down the hall; singles are boxlike but cheap. No credit cards. €40, en suite €50.

Port Vell

Grand Marina World Trade Centre, Moll de Barcelona ☎936 039 000, ⊛www.grandmarinahotel.com. Five-star comforts on eight floors overlooking the port. Most of the rooms have enormous marble bathrooms with jacuzzi baths and a separate dressing area. Public areas draw gasps, with commissioned works by Catalan artists and a rooftop pool with fantastic views. Winter-season and other special rates sometimes bring the price down to under €200; otherwise, from €300.

El Raval and around

Australia Ronda Universitat 11, 4° ☎933 174 177, ⊛www.residenciaustralia.com. The voluble Maria is well into her third decade looking after visitors, and treats everyone kindly. The place is a bit old-fashioned and a bit eccentric – you can only go up in the elevator, not down (don't ask). There's one single and six doubles, or a more spacious one-bed suite with lounge, fridge and coffee-making machine in the next block of the Ronda. €50, en suite €60, suite €65.

Cèntric c/Casanova 13 ☎934 267 573 or 902 014 881, ⊛www.hostalcentric.com. Most rooms feature new panelling and furniture, decent beds and plenty of light; cheaper ones on the upper floors (no elevator) share bathrooms, while some of the more expensive ones also have air conditioning. There's a sunny terrace at the rear and Internet access. €60, en suite from €80.

Duques de Bergara c/de Bergara 11 ☎933 015 151, ⊛www.hoteles-catalonia.es. Handsome late nineteenth-century building whose rooms have a bright, contemporary air, with parquet floors, brown marble bathrooms and little sitting areas – upgrade to a junior suite and you get jet-black marble and a jacuzzi bath, lounge area and huge TV. It's set in a small side street a few minutes from El Raval, but there are Catalunya views from some balconies, and a small first-floor outdoor pool and deck. From €180.

Gat Raval c/Joaquín Costa 44, 2° ☎934 816 670, ⊛www.gataccommodation .com. Boutique style on a budget – folding chair, wall-mounted TV, and signature backlit street photograph/artwork that doubles as a reading light. Only six of the 24 rooms are en suite, but communal facilities are good, and there's Internet access and free tea and coffee. At the nearby sister hotel, *Gat Xino*, c/Hospital 149–155, all the rooms are en suite and breakfast is included. €66, en suite €75, *Gat Xino* €100.

Gravina c/Gravina 12 ☎933 016 868, ⊛www.hotelh10gravina.com. The old-style facade deceives, for this is a contemporary update and good value for money. It's fairly quiet (off the main road), while comfort levels are high – toiletries, robes and hairdryers in the bathrooms, neat little window-side armchairs, artwork in the sharply styled public areas, and a buffet breakfast included in the price. From €150.

Grau c/Ramelleres 27 ☎933 018 135, ⊛www.hostalgrau.com. A really friendly place, whose centrally heated rooms on several floors (no elevator) have new beds, freshly painted walls and shutters. There's a little lounge area with Internet access, plus a good choice of breakfasts (not included) served in the adjacent bar. Six small private apartments in the same building (sleeping 2, 3 or 4, available by the night) offer a bit more independence. €55, en suite €70, apartments from €80.

Meson Castilla c/Valldonzella 5 ☎933 182 182, ⊛www.husa.es. A throwback to 1950s rural Spain, with every inch carved, painted and stencilled, from the grandfather clock in reception to the wardrobe in your room. Large, air-conditioned rooms (some with terraces) filled with country furniture, a vast rustic dining room (buffet breakfast included) and – best of all – a lovely tiled rear patio on which to relax in the sun. From €120.

Peninsular c/de Sant Pau 34 ☎933 023 138, ⊕934 123 699. The building originally belonging to a priestly order, which explains

the slightly cell-like quality of the rooms. There's nothing spartan about the attractive galleried inner courtyard (around which the rooms are ranged), hung with dozens of plants, while breakfast (included) is served in the arcaded dining room. €50, en suite €70.

Sant Agustí Pl. Sant Agustí 3 ☎933 181 658, ⊛www.hotelsa.com. Barcelona's oldest hotel is housed in a former seventeenth-century convent building, with balconies overlooking a restored square and namesake church. The appealing rooms have been modernized and air-conditioned, with the best located right in the attic (supplement charged), from where there are rooftop views. Breakfast included. From €145.

Terrassa c/Junta del Comerç 11 ☎933 025 174, ⊕933 012 188. Clean and friendly backpackers' favourite, with plain rooms with a partition shower-toilet – those at the back overlook a large sunny terrace, open to all guests. However, prices may rise as the owners are putting in proper bathrooms, adding big closets and fitting double-glazed windows onto the street-side balconies. From €40.

La Ribera and Sant Pere

Banys Orientals c/de l'Argenteria 37 ☎932 688 460, ⊛www .hotelbanysorientals.com. Funky boutique hotel with classy rooms. Hardwood floors, crisp white sheets, sharp marble bathrooms and urban-chic decor – not to mention the bargain prices for this sort of style – make it a hugely popular choice. The attached restaurant, *Senyor Parellada*, is a great find too. €100.

Nuevo Colón Avgda. Marquès de l'Argentera 19, 1° ☎933 195 077, ⊛www.hostalnuevocolon.com. In the hands of the same friendly family for over seventy years, with 26 spacious rooms painted yellow and kitted out with directors' chairs, good beds and double glazing. Front rooms are very sunny, as is the lounge and terrace, all with side views to Ciutadella park. There are also three self-catering apartments available (by the night) in the same building, which sleep up to six. €45, en suite €55, apartments €150.

Pensió 2000 c/Sant Pere Més Alt 6, 1° ☎ 933 107 466, ⊛ www.pensio2000.com. As close to a family-style bed and breakfast as Barcelona gets – seven huge rooms in a welcoming mansion apartment strewn with books, plants and pictures. A third person could easily share most rooms (€18 extra), while a choice of breakfasts (not included) is served either in your room or on the internal patio. €50, en suite €65.

Port Olímpic

Arts Barcelona c/Marina 19–21 ☎ 900 221 900 or 932 211 000, ⊛ www.ritzcarlton.com/hotels/barcelona. See map on p.118. Thirty-three floors of five-star designer luxury, with fabulous views of the port and sea. Service and standards are first-rate (there's a team of butlers on call) and the sharply styled rooms are highly pleasing, with floor-to-ceiling windows, thick carpets and robes, enormous marble bathrooms and fresh flowers. The seafront gardens encompass an open-air pool and hot tub, while two fine restaurants, a terrace café, gym and sauna complete the lineup. Special rates start at around €200; otherwise, from €400.

Eixample

Balmes c/Mallorca 216 ☎ 934 511 914, ⊛ www.derbyhotels.es. Agreeable boutique hotel with sharp-as-a-knife dining and bar facilities, and classy rooms with parquet floors and leather sofas. A couple of ground-floor rooms have their own terrace overlooking the lush patio garden, complete with swimming pool and bar, and on your way in and out every day you get to browse the African art and sculpture in the lobby. From €250.

Claris c/Pau Claris 150 ☎ 934 876 262, ⊛ www.derbyhotels.es. Very select, very palatial, from the incense-scented marble lobby complete with authentic Roman

mosaics to the hugely appealing rooms ranged around a soaring, water-washed atrium. And how many hotels have their own private antiquities museum? The staff couldn't be more accommodating, there's a rooftop terrace pool for those idle moments, a great bar and one of the best hotel restaurants in the city. From €350.

Condes de Barcelona Pg. de Gràcia 73–75 ☎934 674 780, ⏾www .condesdebarcelona.com. Straddling two sides of c/Mallorca, the *Condes* is fashioned from two former palaces, its rooms all turned out in contemporary style, some with jacuzzi and balcony, some with views of Gaudí's La Pedrera. Best deal are those on the south side, seventh floor exterior, with fantastic private terraces but charging standard room rates. There's also a roof terrace and plunge pool, bar and restaurant. From €250.

D'Uxelles Gran Via de les Corts Catalanes 688 ☎932 652 560, ⏾www.hotelduxelles.com. The elegant nineteenth-century town-house rooms feature wrought-iron bedsteads, typical tiled floors and Andalucian-style bathrooms, and some also have balconies and little private patios (it's quietest at the back of the building). Prices are highly reasonable, and extra beds can be placed in many rooms – a few rooms are also available in another building at Gran Via 667. €100.

Ginebra Rambla de Catalunya 1, 3° ☎933 171 063, ✉hotelginebra@telefonica .net. Good-sized rooms with nice old furniture, bathrooms you can turn round in for a change, pot plants, cappuccino machine and small bar. All rooms come with TV and air conditioning, and some have impressive views of Plaça de Catalunya – ask for one of the four with a balcony. €75.

Girona c/Girona 24, 1° ☎932 650 259, ⏾www.hostalgirona.com. The entrance has a positively baronial stairway and things are scarcely any less impressive inside the family-run building – a wide range of cosy rooms (some sharing a bathroom, others with a shower or full bath), corridors laid with rugs, polished wooden doors, paintings and restored furniture. From €46, full en suite €55.

Goya c/de Pau Claris 74, 1° ☎933 022 565, ⏾www.hostalgoya.com. Upgraded

mansion-building with a dozen older-style rooms and seven more on the "principal" floor below, which have been fitted with laminate flooring, air conditioning, stylish bed linen and modern bathrooms – the three largest (and most expensive, at €90) open directly onto a terrace. There are sitting areas, and free coffee and tea available, on both floors. €55, en suite €65/75.

Granvia Gran Via de les Corts Catalanes 642 ☎933 181 900, ⏾www.nnhotels.es. An attractive town house built for a nineteenth-century banking family, with grand public rooms exuding old-style comfort. You may be less lucky with your own room, as some of the accommodation is cramped, but there's a nice roof terrace. Prices are pretty reasonable too, given that air conditioning, full bath and satellite TV come as standard. €120.

Majestic Pg. de Gràcia 68 ☎934 881 717, ⏾www.hotelmajestic.es. Big, traditional hotel, refitted in muted colours to provide a tranquil base. Objets and limited-edition art adorn the public areas, and the rooms – bigger than many in this price range – have been pleasantly refurbished, but the absolute clincher is the rooftop pool and deck, with amazing views over the rooftops to the Sagrada Família. The restaurant is excellent too. From €320.

Oliva Pg. de Gràcia 32, 4° ☎934 881 789 or 934 880 162, ⏾www.lasguias .com/hostaloliva. Ride the antique elevator to the top floor for an Eixample bargain – marble floors, high ceilings and plenty of light in rooms that have been freshly decorated with a bit of zest. If you want a balcony and a view, be warned that the noise permeates, even at these rarefied levels. No credit cards. €50, en suite €60.

Omm c/Rosselló 265 ☎934 454 000, ⏾www.hotelomm.es. Barcelona's most fashionable restaurant group, Tragaluz, has entered the hotel game with the designer experience that is *Omm* – sixty elegantly presented rooms in muted colours with open-plan bathrooms, a studiously chic bar and restaurant, terrace and pool, and fearsomely handsome staff. From €300.

Paseo de Gràcia Pg. de Gràcia 102 ☎932 155 824, ☎932 153 724. Some might find this funereal, others will delight in its faded 1950s charm – the lounge, in particular, is an untouched relic of bygone days. Rooms, too, have yet to see a renovator, which means ageing tiling and furniture, but prices are pitched accordingly. Some rooms on the upper floors have terraces and city views, but you can't book these in advance. €75.

Prestige Pg. de Gràcia 62 ☎932 724 180, ✆www.prestigepaseodegracia.com. A sharp redesign of a 1930s Eixample building has added achingly fashionable minimalist rooms, an Oriental-style internal patio garden and the Zeroom, a lounge with wireless Internet facility and style library. It's almost a parody of itself it's so cool, but the staff keep things real and are very helpful. "Functional" (ie standard) rooms are a bit less impressive, so upgrade if you can. From €200.

Regente Rambla de Catalunya 76 ☎934 875 989, ✆www.hcchotels.es. They've restored the *modernista* facade and kept the decorative panelling and stained glass; together with the rooftop pool, garden terrace and funky bar, that's some attraction. But even the hotel recommends an internal room to escape the street noise, so it's best to book a rear top-floor room with private green-baize terrace and city views. These are the same price as other rooms but go quickly. €180.

Ritz Gran Via de les Corts Catalanes 668 ☎935 101 130, ✆www.ritzbcn.com. Formally attired staff jump to your every command, while your domain extends to opulent lounges, a terrace-garden, bar, restaurant and health club. The suites are sensational, but for these – as for the deluxe rooms (there's no such thing as "standard" at the *Ritz*) – you're paying crazily inflated prices. From €400.

Rondas c/Girona 4, 3° ☎932 325 102. A cheap choice with a friendly English-speaking welcome and a touch of domesticity – an old carved bed in one room, the share of a balcony onto the street in another. Good for lone travellers, as there are four singles (€30); otherwise, six cramped doubles available, some with attached shower and toilet. No credit cards. €40, en suite €45.

Windsor Rambla de Catalunya 84 ☎932 151 198. Genteel place with English-speaking management, set in a lovingly furnished building on the Eixample's nicest avenue. There are fifteen rooms, all with en-suite shower and toilet (and often booked long in advance). No credit cards. €70.

Youth hostels

Although there are lots of hostels in Barcelona, you should always make an advance reservation as most of them are very popular. Internet access, kitchens, common/games rooms and laundry facilities are standard – always use the lockers or safes provided (for which there's sometimes a small charge). You need an International Youth Hostel Federation (IYHF) card for a couple of the hostels, but you can join on checkin. The only tourist office to handle youth hostel bookings is at Barcelona Sants (see box p.75). Unless otherwise stated, the hostels below are marked on the map on pp.176–177.

Albergue Verge de Montserrat Pg. de la Mare de Déu del Coll 41–51, Horta ☎932 105 151, ✆www.tujuca.com. Not on map. Converted mansion with gardens, terrace and city views – a long way out, but close to Parc Güell (m Vallcarca and 10min walk, or bus #28 from Pl. de Catalunya). Multi-bedded dorms sleep 4, 6, 8 and 12, with local restaurant just around the corner or meals provided. IYHF membership required; five-night maximum stay. €23 includes breakfast, low season €19.

Barcelona Mar c/de Sant Pau 80, El Raval ☎933 248 530, ✉www.youthostel-barcelona.com. Large hostel with mixed dorms – in 6-, 8-, 10-, 14- or 16-bedded rooms – on the fringe of the Rambla de Raval. It's a secure place, with 24hr reception. €23 includes breakfast, low season €18–20.

Center Ramblas c/Hospital 63, El Raval ☎934 124 069, ✉www.center-ramblas.com. Very popular 200-bed hostel, given its location 100m from the Ramblas, and well equipped with 3- to 10-bed dorms, lounge, bar and travel library. Open 24hr. IYHF membership required. No credit cards. Under-26s €15.50, over 26s €20, includes breakfast.

Gothic Point c/Vigatans 5, La Ribera ☎932 687 808, ✉www.gothicpoint.com. A grand downstairs communal area shows off the building's dramatic proportions, and on the roof there's mini-golf. Rooms have 14 bunks and attached bathrooms, and each bed gets its own bedside cabinet and reading light. Bike rental available. Open 24hr. €21 includes breakfast, low season €18.

Itaca c/Ripoll 21, Barri Gòtic ☎933 019 751, ✉www.itacahostel.com. Bright and breezy house close to the cathedral with unusually spacious rooms (sleeping 8 or 12) with balconies. Dorms are mixed, though there is a six-bed women-only dorm and one double room (€50, low season €44) available. No TV lounge, but a kitchen, coffee machine and choice of three €2 breakfasts. €21, low season €18.

Kabul Pl. Reial 17, Barri Gòtic ☎933 185 190, ✉www.kabul-hostel.com. A budget travellers' haven in the heart of the old town – open 24hr, with a good notice board, pool table and terrace, and weekly pub crawls to help you get acquainted. A big, monastic-style common room/bar overlooks the square. It has reputation as a bit of a party place, but it's safe and welcoming enough. Rooms vary in size and number of beds and are priced accordingly. €17–24, low season €14–17, includes breakfast.

Sea Point Pl. del Mar 1–4, Barceloneta ☎932 247 075, ✉www.seapointhostel.com. See map on p.74 Neat little modern bunk rooms sleeping 6 or 7, with an integral shower-bathroom in each one. The attached café, where you have breakfast, looks right out onto the boardwalk and palm trees. Bike rental available. Open 24hr. €21 includes breakfast, low season €18.

Essentials

Arrival

Whatever your point of arrival, it's easy to get to central Barcelona. In most cases, you can be off the plane, train or bus and in your hotel room within the hour.

By air

Barcelona's **airport** at El Prat de Llobregat (☎902 400 550, ✆www.aena.es) is 12km southwest of the city. Easyjet uses Terminal A, British Airways and Iberia Terminal B. There's a tourist office in each terminal, handling hotel bookings; there are also ATMs, exchange facilities and car rental offices.

A metered **taxi** to the centre costs €20–25, including the airport surcharge (and note other surcharges for travel after 10pm, at weekends or for luggage in the boot). Far cheaper is the **airport train** (6.13am–10.43pm; journey time 18min; €2.25; info on ☎902 240 202), which runs every thirty minutes to Barcelona Sants (see "By rail and road" below) and continues on to Plaça de Catalunya (best stop for the Ramblas and Barri Gòtic) and Arc de Triomf (for La Ribera). There are metro stations at each of these stops too.

Alternatively, the **Aerobús** service (Mon–Fri 5.30am–11pm, Sat & Sun 6am–11.30pm; €3.45) leaves every twelve minutes, stopping in the city at Plaça d'Espanya, Plaça Universitat, Plaça de Catalunya and Passeig de Gràcia. It takes around thirty minutes to reach Plaça de Catalunya, though allow longer in the rush hour.

By rail and road

The national rail service is operated by RENFE (fare and timetable information on ☎902 240 202, ✆www.renfe.es). The city's main station is **Barcelona Sants**, 3km west of the centre, with a metro station (called m Sants Estació) that links directly to the Ramblas (m Liceu), Plaça de Catalunya and Passeig de Gràcia. Some Spanish intercity services and international trains also stop at **Estació de França**, 1km east of the Ramblas and close to m Barceloneta.

Regional and local commuter train services are operated by FGC (☎932 051 515, ✆www.fgc.es), with stations at **Plaça de Catalunya**, at the top of the Ramblas (for trains from the airport and from coastal towns north of the city); **Plaça d'Espanya** (Montserrat); and **Passeig de Gràcia** (Catalunya provincial destinations).

The main bus terminal is the **Estació del Nord** (☎932 656 508; m Arc de Triomf), three blocks north of Parc de la Ciutadella. Some intercity buses also make a stop at the bus terminal behind Barcelona Sants station, while international buses tend to stop only at Barcelona Sants. Either way, you're only a short metro ride from the city centre.

With a car, the best advice is to head straight for a signposted central **car park** (from €1.60 per hr, or €17.50–20 for 24hr), which include those at Plaça de Catalunya, Plaça Urquinaona, Arc de Triomf, Passeig de Gràcia, Plaça dels Angels/MACBA and Avinguda Paral.lel. It can be tough to find **street parking**, especially in the old town (where it's nearly all residents' parking only). In the Eixample the ubiquitous blue meter-zones are for pay-and-display parking, usually with a two-hour maximum stay.

Information

The city's tourist board, **Turisme de Barcelona** (☎807 117 222 from within Spain, ☎932 853 834 from abroad, ✆www.barcelonaturisme.com), has useful offices on arrival at the airport and Barcelona Sants. The main city office is in **Plaça de Catalunya** (daily 9am–9pm; m Catalunya), down the steps in the southeast corner of the square, where there's a money exchange service and separate accommodation desk. There's also an office in the Barri Gòtic at **Plaça de Sant Jaume**, entrance at c/Ciutat 2 (Mon–Fri 9am–8pm, Sat 10am–8pm, Sun & hols 10am–2pm; m Jaume I).

For information about travelling in the wider province of Catalunya, you need the Centre d'Informació de Catalunya at **Palau Robert**, Pg. de Gràcia 107, Eixample, m Diagonal (☏932 384 000, ⊛www.gencat.net/probert; Mon–Sat 10am–7.30pm, Sun & hols 10am–2.30pm).

For anything else you might need to know, try the city's ☏**010 telephone enquiries service** (Mon–Sat 8am–10pm; some English-speaking staff available). They'll be able to help with questions about transport, public services and other matters.

Events, concerts, exhibitions and festivals are covered in full at the walk-in office of the Institut de Cultura at the **Palau de la Virreina**, Ramblas 99, m Liceu (☏933 017 775, ⊛www .bcn.es/cultura; Mon–Sat 10am–8pm, Sun 11am–3pm). The most useful **list-ings magazine** is the paperback-book-sized, Spanish-language *Guia del Ocio* (out every Thursday; ⊛www .guiadelociobcn.es), available at kiosks all over the city.

Our maps will guide you around the city, though for an excellent tough, waterproof **street plan** with full practical information and listings, look no further than *Barcelona: The Rough Guide Map*.

Barcelona on the Internet

The city tourist office website (⊛www.barcelonaturisme.com) is a good place to start and, along with those operated by the city hall (Ajuntament; ⊛www.bcn.es) and local government (Generalitat; ⊛www.gencat.es), has a full English-language version. From these three alone you'll be able to find out museum opening hours, bus routes, local politics, all-night pharmacies, festivals, sports, theatres and much, much more. The sites listed below offer more specialized information.

⊛**www.barcelona-on-line.es** Packed with information in English on Barcelona, with searchable listings and an entertainment guide.

⊛**www.catalanencyclopaedia.com** English-language online encyclopedia, for full information about all matters Catalan.

⊛**www.gaudiclub.com** The best first stop

Discount cards

If you're going to do a lot of sightseeing, you can save yourself money by buying one of the available discount cards.

• **Barcelona Card** (1 day €16.25, 2 days €19.25, 3 days €22.25, 4 days €24 or 5 days €26). Free public transport, plus museum and attraction discounts. Available at the Plaça de Catalunya and airport tourist offices, Estació del Nord bus station and other outlets.

• **Articket** (€15; valid three months; ⊛www.articketbcn.com). Half-price admission into six major art galleries (including MNAC, MACBA, and Tàpies and Miró foundations). Buy it at participating galleries, or at Plaça de Catalunya or Barcelona Sants tourist office.

• **Ruta del Modernisme** (€12; valid one year; ⊛www.rutamodernisme.com). Glossy English-language guide and map, containing vouchers for significant discounts to most major *modernista* sites and attractions (including Sagrada Família and La Pedrera), plus other benefits. Available in city bookshops and at the Centre del Modernisme outlets in Casa Amatller (Eixample, p.124) and Hospital de la Santa Creu i de Sant Pau (Sagrada Família and Glòries, p.136).

for Antoni Gaudí and his works, with plenty of links to other sites.

⊛www.intercat.gencat.es/guia The University of Barcelona's online English–Catalan phrase book, with an audio option.

⊛www.paginasamarillas.es The Spanish Yellow Pages (find any business in Barcelona), with links to the *Paginas Blancas* (White Pages – find a person) and a Barcelona street-finder.

⊛www.rutadisseny.com Designer guide to the city's most cutting-edge shops, bars, restaurants and buildings, with maps, reviews and walking itineraries.

City transport and tours

Barcelona's excellent integrated transport system comprises the metro, buses and local trains, plus a network of funiculars and cable cars. Detailed transport information is available by telephone (☎010) and in English on the Internet (⊛www.tmb.net), and there's an invaluable free public transport map (*Guia d'Autobusos Urbans de Barcelona*), available at TMB customer service centres at Barcelona Sants station, and Diagonal, Sagrada Família and Universitat metro stations. The map and ticket information is also posted at major bus stops and all metro stations. There's no need to rent a car to see anything in the city, while daytrips to Sitges (p.168) and Montserrat (p.164) are best undertaken anyway by public transport.

Tickets and travel passes

On all the city's public transport you can buy a **single ticket** every time you ride (€1.10), but it's much cheaper to buy a **targeta** – a discount ticket strip. They are available at metro and train stations, but not on the buses. The best general deal is the **T-10** ("tay day-oo" in Catalan) *targeta* (€6), valid for ten separate journeys, with changes between methods of transport allowed within 75 minutes. The ticket can also be used by more than one person at a time – punch it the same number of times as there are people travelling.

Other useful (single-person) *targetes* include: the **T-Dia** ("tay dee-ah"; 1 day's unlimited travel; €4.60), plus combos up to the **5-Dies** (5 days; €18.20); the **T-50/30** (50 trips within a 30-day period; €25); or the **T-Mes** (1 month; €38.80). Prices given above are for passes valid as far as the Zone 1 city limits, which in practice is everywhere you're likely to want to go except the airport, Montserrat and Sitges. For single trips to these and other out-of-town destinations, it's best to buy a specific ticket.

The metro

The quickest way of getting around Barcelona is by metro. Entrances are marked with a red diamond sign with an "M". Its **hours of operation** are Monday to Thursday 5am to midnight; Friday, Saturday and the day before a public holiday 5am to 2am; Sunday and public holidays 6am to midnight. The system is perfectly safe, though many of the train carriages are heavily graffitied. Buskers and beggars are common, zipping from one carriage to the next at stations.

Buses and trains

Most **buses** operate daily, roughly from 4 or 5am until 10.30pm. **Night buses** (*autobusos nocturns* or simply *Nitbus*) fill in the gaps on all the main routes, with services every twenty to sixty minutes from around 10pm to 4am.

The FGC **commuter train line** has its main stations at Plaça de Catalunya and Plaça d'Espanya. You'll use this going to Sarrià, Vallvidrera, Tibidabo and Montserrat, and details are given in the text where appropriate. The national rail service, RENFE, runs all the other services out of

Barcelona, with local lines designated as **Rodiales/Cercanías**. The hub is Barcelona Sants station, with services also passing through Plaça de Catalunya (heading north) and Passeig de Gràcia (south).

Funiculars, tram and cable cars

Several **funicular railways** still operate in the city, most notably to Montjuïc (see p.112) and Tibidabo (p.160). Weekend visits to Tibidabo also combine a funicular trip with a ride on the antique tram, the **Tramvia Blau** (p.160). There are two **cable-car** (*telefèric*) rides you can make: from Barceloneta across the harbour to Montjuïc (see p.78), and then from the top station of the Montjuïc funicular right the way up to the castle (p.113).

Taxis

Black-and-yellow **taxis** are inexpensive and plentiful. There's a minimum charge of €1.15 (€1.30 after 10pm, weekends and holidays) and after that it's currently €0.69/0.88 per kilometre. Most short journeys across town run to around €6. There are taxi ranks outside major train and metro stations, in main squares, near large hotels and at places along the main avenues. To call a taxi in advance (few of the operators speak English, and you'll be charged around an extra €3), try **Barna Taxis** ☎933 577 755, **Fono-Taxi** ☎933 001 100, **Radio Taxi Barcelona** ☎932 250 000, **Radio Taxi 033** ☎933 033 033, **Servi-Taxi** ☎933 300 300, or **Taxi Amic** ☎934 208 088.

City tours

Two main tour-bus operators feature daily board-at-will, open-top services (1 day €16, 2 days €20), which can drop you outside every attraction in the city. The choice is between **Barcelona Tours** or the **Bus Turístic**, with frequent departures from Plaça de Catalunya and many other stops – tickets are available on board.

Advance booking is advised (at Pl. de Catalunya tourist office) for **Barcelona Walking Tours'** ninety-minute historical Barri Gòtic tour (Sat & Sun all year, in English at 10am; plus April–Sept Thurs & Fri at 10am; €8). There's also a "Picasso Tour" (Sat & Sun all year, in English at 10.30am; €10).

The guides at **My Favourite Things** (☎933 295 351 or 637 265 405, ⊛www.myft.net) reveal Barcelona in a new light, particularly on the signature tour "My Favourite Fusion", which gives an insider's view of the city. Tours (in English, flexible departures, call for information) cost €25 per person and last around four hours, and there's always time for diversions, workshop visits and café stops.

The **Travel Bar** at c/Boqueria 27, Barri Gòtic, ⓜ Liceu (☎933 425 252, ⊛www.travelbar.com), organizes a variety of youth-oriented tours, including an evening bar crawl (€26), tapas bar tour (€33), bike tour (€58) and kayaking on the harbour (June–Sept only; €23). There are also city bike tours (March to mid-Dec 1–2 daily; €22) with **Fat Tire Bike Tours** (☎933 013 612, ⊛www.fattirebiketoursbarcelona.com) and others, including Un Coxte Menys (see "Directory: Bike rental" on p.192).

To see Barcelona from the sea, go with **Las Golondrinas** (☎934 423 106, ⊛www.lasgolondrinas.com), whose daily sightseeing boats depart (at least hourly June–Sept; less frequently Oct–May) from the quayside opposite the Columbus statue, at the bottom of the Ramblas (ⓜ Drassanes), and visit either the port (35min; €3.50), or port and local coast (1hr 30min; €8.50).

Catamaran Orsom (☎932 258 260, ⊛www.barcelona-orsom.com) has three daily afternoon departures (€12) from the same quayside – there's a ticket kiosk there, or phone and reserve the day before. The catamaran also has a summer evening jazz cruise (daily June, July & Aug; €12).

Festivals and events

Almost any month you visit Barcelona you'll coincide with a festival, event or holiday. The best are picked out below, but for a full list call into the Palau de la Virreina (see p.53), or check out the Ajuntament (city hall) website ⊛www.bcn.es.

Dia de Sant Jordi

St George's Day (**April 23**) celebrates Catalunya's patron saint, with hundreds of book and flower stalls down the Ramblas, on Passàg de Gràcia and in Plaça de Sant Jaume.

Marató de l'Espectacle

Every **June** or **July** it's time for the annual Entertainment Marathon (⊛www.marato.com), a nonstop, two-day festival of local theatre, dance, mime, cabaret, music and children's shows, which takes place at the Mercat de les Flors theatre.

Verbena/Dia de Sant Joan

The "eve" and "day" of St John (**June 23/24**) herald probably the wildest celebrations in the city, with a "night of fire" of bonfires and fireworks (particularly on Montjuïc), drinking and dancing, and watching the sun come up on the beach. The day itself (June 24) is a public holiday.

Sónar

Sónar (⊛www.sonar.es), Europe's biggest and most cutting-edge electronic music and multimedia art festival, presents three days of brilliant noise and spectacle every **June**. Experience DJs, VDJs, gigs, conferences, exhibitions and installations at venues across the city.

Festival del Grec

Starting in the last week of **June** (and running throughout July and into August), the Grec performing arts festival (⊛www.bcn.es/grec) incorporates theatre, music and dance, some of it free, much of it performed at Montjuïc's Teatre Grec (see p.110).

Festa Major de Gràcia

A mid- to late-**August** extravaganza (⊛www.festamajordegracia.org) of music, dancing, decorated floats and streets, noisy fireworks, parades of giants and devils, and human castle-building takes place in the streets and squares of Barcelona's most vibrant neighbourhood. The festivities last a week – don't miss them if you're in town.

Festa de la Mercè

The city's main festival (⊛www.bcn.es/merce) – dedicated to Our Lady of Mercy – is celebrated for several days around **September 24** (with the 24th a public holiday). There are live bands and traditional dancing outside the cathedral and in central squares, plus a parade of costumed giants and fire-running devils, a breathtaking firework display choreographed to music, human tower competitions, and road and bike races.

Festival de Jazz

The annual jazz festival in **October/November** attracts big-name solo artists and bands to the clubs, as well as smaller-scale street concerts.

Christmas

For more than two hundred years the Christmas season has seen a special market and crafts fair, the **Fira de Santa Llúcia** (Dec 1–22), outside the cathedral. Browse for gifts, or watch the locals snapping up Christmas trees, nativity figures and traditional decorations.

New Year

At **Cap d'Any** (New Year's Eve) there are mass gatherings in Plaça de Catalunya and other main squares. You're supposed to eat 12 grapes in the last 12 seconds of the year for 12 months of good luck. The Three Kings (who traditionally distribute seasonal gifts to Spanish children) arrive by sea at the port at about 5pm on January 5 and undertake the **Cavalcada de Reis**, riding into town, throwing sweets as they go. The traditional gift-giving is the next day (Jan 6).

ESSENTIALS Festivals and events

Directory

AIRPORT Trains to the airport depart every 30min from Barcelona Sants (5.43am–10.13pm; €2.25) or Pl. de Catalunya (6.08am–10.08pm). Aerobús runs every 12min from Pl. de Catalunya, Pg. de Gràcia or Pl. d'Espanya (Mon–Fri 6am–midnight, Sat & Sun 6.30am–midnight; €3.45).

BANKS AND EXCHANGE Normal **banking hours** are Monday to Friday from 8.30am to 2pm. Outside these hours you can use an **exchange office**, including those at the airport (daily 7.30am–10.45pm), Barcelona Sants (daily 8am–10pm), El Corte Inglés (Mon–Sat 10am–9.30pm), and the Pl. de Catalunya tourist office (Mon–Sat 9am–9pm, Sun 9am–2pm). However, by far the easiest way to get money is to use your bank debit card to withdraw cash from an **ATM**, found all over the city, including the airport and major train stations. You can usually withdraw up to €300 a day and instructions are offered in English once you insert your card.

BIKE RENTAL Half-day rental costs around €10–15, full-day €25, from: **Biciclot**, Pg. Marítim 33–35, Port Olímpic, m Ciutadella-Vila Olímpica ☎932 219 778, ⊛www. biciclot.net; **Bicitram**, Avgda. Marquès de l'Argentera 15, La Ribera, m Barceloneta ☎607 226 069 or 636 401 997 (weekends & hols only); **Decathlon**, Pl. Villa de Madrid 1–3, Barri Gòtic, m Catalunya ☎933 426 161; **Scenic**, c/Marina 22, Port Olímpic, m Ciutadella-Vila Olímpica ☎932 211 666; **Un Coxte Menys**, c/Esparteria 3, La Ribera m Barceloneta ☎932 682 105, ⊛www.bicicletabarcelona.com.

CINEMA Films at most of the larger cinemas and multiplexes (including the Maremàgnum screens at Port Vell) are usually shown dubbed into Spanish or Catalan. However, several cinemas do show original-language (*versión original* or "V.O.") foreign films, and are listed in the week's *Guía del Ocio*. Tickets cost around €6, while most cinemas have discounted entry one night (usually Mon or Wed), costing around €4. Many also feature late-night weekend screenings (*madrugadas*), at 12.30 or 1am. Best art-house cinema is the Generalitat's Filmoteca (see p.141).

CONSULATES Australia, Gran Via Carles III 98, Les Corts, m Maria Cristina/Les Corts ☎934 909 013, ⊛www.embaustralia.es; **Britain**, Avgda. Diagonal 477, Eixample,

m Hospital Clínic ☎933 666 200, ⊛www.ukinspain.com; **Canada**, c/Elisenda de Pinós 10, Sarrià, FGC Reina Elisenda ☎932 042 700, ⊛www.canada-es.org; **Republic of Ireland**, Gran Via Carles III 94, Les Corts, m Maria Cristina/Les Corts ☎934 915 021; **New Zealand**, Trav. de Gràcia 64, Gràcia, FGC Gràcia ☎932 090 399; **USA**, Pg. de la Reina Elisenda 23, Sarrià, FGC Reina Elisenda ☎932 802 227, ⊛www.embusa.es.

CRIME To avoid petty crime: sling bags across your body, not off one shoulder; don't carry wallets in zipped or back pockets; and don't hang bags on the back of a café chair. Make photocopies of your passport, leaving the original and any tickets in the hotel safe. The crowded Ramblas and the medieval streets to either side are where you most need to be on your guard – keep a hand on your wallet or bag if it appears you're being distracted. However, don't be unduly paranoid. The potential for violent street crime is much lower than in British and US cities.

DISABLED TRAVELLERS Barcelona's airport and Aerobús are fully accessible to travellers in wheelchairs. The metro is more problematic since only line 2 is easily accessible, with elevators at major stations (including Pg. de Gràcia and Sagrada Família) from the street to the platforms. However, many city buses have been adapted for wheelchair use, with automatic ramps/steps and a designated wheelchair space inside. The **Institut Municipal de Disminuïts** (c/Llacuna 161, 3° ☎932 918 400; m Llacuna) produces an accessibility booklet, *Guia d'Accessibilitat*, available from tourist offices, though if you're coming for the showpiece attractions, note that only the Fundació Joan Miró, Fundació Antoni Tàpies, La Pedrera, Caixa Forum, Museu de la Ciència, Museu d'Història de Catalunya and Palau de la Música are fully accessible; most old-town attractions, including the Museu Picasso, have steps or other impediments to access. The city information line – ☎010 – also has accessibility information for hotels, restaurants, museums, bars and stores.

EMERGENCY SERVICES Call ☎112 for ambulance, police and fire services; ☎061 for an ambulance.

GAY AND LESBIAN For up-to-date information and other advice, contact the lesbian and gay city telephone hotline on ☏900 601 601 (Mon–Fri 6–10pm only). **Ca la Dona** (c/de Casp 38, Eixample ☏934 127 161, ✆www.caladona.pangea.org; m Urquinaona), a women's centre with library and bar, is used for meetings of feminist and lesbian organizations; information available to callers. General listings magazine *Guia del Ocio* can put you on the right track for bars and clubs, though there's also a good free magazine called *Nois*, widely available in bars and clubs, which carries an up-to-date review of the scene. For full listings and other links, the Web portal ✆www.gaybarcelona.net is extremely useful. The annual lesbian and gay pride march is on the nearest Saturday to June 28.

HOSPITALS The following central hospitals have 24hr accident and emergency services: **Centre Perecamps**, Avgda. Drassanes 13–15, El Raval, m Drassanes ☏934 410 600; **Hospital Clínic i Provincial**, c/Villarroel 170, Eixample, m Hospital Clínic ☏932 275 400; **Hospital del Mar**, Pg. Marítim 25–29, Vila Olímpica, m Ciutadella-Vila Olímpica ☏932 489 011; **Hospital de la Santa Creu i de Sant Pau**, c/Sant Antoni Maria Claret, Eixample, m Hospital de Sant Pau ☏932 919 000.

INTERNET ACCESS There are Internet places all over Barcelona, and competition has driven prices down to around €1 an hour.

LEFT LUGGAGE Barcelona Sants office (daily 7am–11pm; €3–4.50 a day). Lockers at Estació de França, Passeig de Gràcia station and Estació del Nord (all 6am–11.30pm; €3–4.50 a day).

LOST PROPERTY The main lost property office (*objectes perduts*) is at c/de la Ciutat 9, Barri Gòtic, m Jaume I (Mon–Fri 9.30am–1.30pm; ☏934 023 161). You could also try the transport office at m Universitat station.

MAIL The **main post office** (*Correus*) is on Pl. d'Antoni López, at the eastern end of Pg. de Colom, in the Barri Gòtic (Mon–Sat 8.30am–9.30pm, Sun 8.30am–2.30pm; ☏902 197 197, ✆www.correos.es; m Barceloneta/Jaume I). There's a poste restante/general delivery service here (*llista de correus*), plus express post, fax service and phone-card sales. Each city neighbourhood also has a post office, though these have far less comprehensive opening hours and services. For **stamps** it's much easier to visit a tobacconist (look for the brown-and-yellow *tabac* sign), found on virtually every street. Use the yellow on-street **postboxes** and put your mail in the flap marked

províncies i estranger or *altres destins*.

MONEY Spain's currency is the **euro** (€), with notes issued in denominations of 5, 10, 20, 50, 100, 200 and 500 euros, and coins in denominations of 1, 2, 5, 10, 20 and 50 cents, and 1 and 2 euros.

NEWSPAPERS AND MAGAZINES Foreign newspapers and magazines are available from the stalls down the Ramblas, on Pg. de Gràcia, on Rambla de Catalunya, around Pl. de Catalunya and at Barcelona Sants. Or try Llibreria Mallorca, Rambla de Catalunya 86, Eixample, m Passeig de Gràcia, which stocks a big selection of British and American newspapers and magazines.

PHARMACIES Usual hours are 9am to 1pm and 4 to 8pm. At least one in each neighbourhood is open 24hr (and marked as such), or phone ☏010 for information on those open out of hours. A list of out-of-hours pharmacies can also be found in the window of each pharmacy store.

POLICE The easiest place to report a crime is at the Guàrdia Urbana (city police) station at Ramblas 43, opposite Pl. Reial, m Liceu ☏933 441 300 (open 24hr; English spoken). If you've had something stolen, you need to go in person for the insurance report to the Policía Nacional office at c/Nou de la Rambla 80, El Raval, m Paral.lel (take your passport).

PUBLIC HOLIDAYS Official holidays are: **January 1** (Cap d'Any, New Year's Day); **January 6** (Epifanía, Epiphany); **Good Friday** & **Easter Monday**; **May 1** (Dia del Treball, May Day/Labour Day); **June 24** (Dia de Sant Joan, St John's Day); **August 15** (L'Assumpció, Assumption of the Virgin); **September 11** (La Diada, Catalan National Day); **September 24** (Festa de la Mercè, Our Lady of Mercè, Barcelona's patron saint); **October 12** (Dia de la Hispanidad, Spanish National Day); **November 1** (Tots Sants, All Saints' Day); **December 6** (Dia de la Constitució, Constitution Day); **December 8** (La Imaculada, Immaculate Conception); **December 25** (Nadal, Christmas Day); **December 26** (Sant Esteve, St Stephen's Day).

TAXES Local sales tax, IVA, is seven percent in hotels and restaurants, and sixteen percent in shops. Quoted prices should always make it clear whether or not tax is included (it usually is).

TELEPHONES Public telephones accept coins, credit cards and phone cards (the latter available in various denominations in tobacconists, newsagents and post offices). The cheapest way to make an international call is to go to a **locutorio** (phone centre), scattered through the old city, particularly in the Raval and Ribera. You'll be assigned a cabin to make your calls, and afterwards you pay in cash.

TICKETS You can buy concert, sporting and exhibition tickets with a credit card using the **ServiCaixa** (☎902 332 211, ✆www.servicaixa.com), automatic dispensing machines in branches of La Caixa savings bank. It's also possible to order tickets by phone or online through *ServiCaixa* or **TelEntrada** (☎902 101 212, ✆www.telentrada.com). In addition, there's a concert ticket desk in the FNAC store, El Triangle, Plaça Catalunya (m Catalunya), while for advance tickets for all Ajuntament-sponsored concerts, visit the Palau de la Virreina, Ramblas 99.

TIME Barcelona is one hour ahead of Greenwich Mean Time (GMT), six hours ahead of New York and Toronto, nine hours ahead of Los Angeles, nine hours behind Sydney and eleven hours behind Auckland. This applies except for brief periods during the changeovers to and from daylight saving (in Spain the clocks go forward in the last week in March, back again in the last week of October).

TIPPING Locals leave only a few cents or round up the change for a coffee or drink, and a euro or two for most meals. Anything beyond is considered excessive, though fancy restaurants may specifically indicate that service is not included, in which case you will be expected to leave ten to fifteen percent. Taxi drivers usually get around five percent, while hotel porters and toilet attendants should be tipped a euro or two.

TRAVEL AGENCIES General travel agencies are found on the Gran Vía de les Corts Catalanes, Pg. de Gràcia, Vía Laietana and the Ramblas. For city tours and local trips, contact **Julia Tours**, Ronda Universitat 5, Eixample, m Universitat ☎933 176 454 or 933 176 209. For youth/student travel contact **Asatej**, Ramblas 140, 5th floor ☎934 126 338, or **Abando**, Ramblas 88–94 ☎933 182 593. The **American Express** office, Pg. de Gràcia 101, Eixample, m Diagonal ☎932 550 000, also has a travel agency.

Budget Barcelona

Here's how to keep costs to a minimum in Barcelona.

• Eat your main meal of the day at lunchtime, when the *menú del día* offers fantastic value.

• Buy a public transport travel pass, which will save you around forty percent on every ride.

• Visit museums and galleries on the first Sunday of the month, when admission is usually free.

• Drink and eat *inside* cafés – there's usually a surcharge for terrace service.

• Take any student/youth/senior citizen cards you're entitled to carry, as they often attract discounts on museum, gallery and attraction charges.

• Take advantage of the discount nights at the cinema (Mon and sometimes Wed) and theatre (Tues).

• Go to the Ramblas, La Seu, Parc de la Ciutadella, Parc del Collserola, Port Olímpic, city beaches, Olympic Stadium, Caixa Forum and Parc Güell – all free.

Language

Catalan

In Barcelona, Catalan (Català) has more or less taken over from Castilian (Castellano) Spanish as the language on street signs and maps. On paper it looks like a cross between French and Spanish and is generally easy to read if you know those two. Few visitors realize how important Catalan is to those who speak it: never commit the error of calling it a dialect! Despite the preponderance of the Catalan language, you'll get by perfectly well in Spanish, as long as you're aware of the use of Catalan in timetables, on menus, and so on. However, you'll generally get a good reception if you at least try communicating in the local language.

Pronunciation

Don't be tempted to use the few rules of Spanish pronunciation you may know – in particular the soft Spanish Z and C don't apply, so unlike in the rest of Spain the city is not Barthelona but Barcelona, as in English.

A as in hat if stressed, as in alone when unstressed.

E varies, but usually as in get.

I as in police.

IG sounds like the "tch" in the English scratch; lleig (ugly) is pronounced "yeah-tch".

O a round full sound, when stressed, otherwise like a soft U sound.

U somewhere between the U of put and rule.

Ç sounds like an English S; plaça is pronounced "plassa".

C followed by an E or I is soft; otherwise hard.

G followed by E or I is like the "zh" in Zhivago; otherwise hard.

H is always silent.

J as in the French "Jean".

L.L is best pronounced (for foreigners) as a single L sound; but for Catalan speakers it has two distinct L sounds.

LL sounds like an English Y or LY, like the "yuh" sound in million.

N as in English, though before F or V it sometimes sounds like an M.

NY corresponds to the Castilian Ñ.

QU before E or I sounds like K, unless the **U** has an umlaut, (Ü) in which case, and before A or O, as in quit.

R is rolled, but only at the start of a word; at the end it's often silent.

T is pronounced as in English, though sometimes it sounds like a D; as in viatge or dotze.

V at the start of a word sounds like B; in all other positions it's a soft F sound.

W is pronounced like a B/V.

X is like SH or CH in most words, though in some, like exit, it sounds like an X.

Z is like the English Z in zoo.

Words and phrases

Basics	
Yes, No, OK	Si, No, Val

Please, Thank you	Si us plau, Gràcies
Hello, Goodbye	Hola, Adéu
Good morning	Bon dia

Good afternoon/night	Bona tarde/nit
See you later	Fins després
Sorry	Ho sento
Excuse me	Perdoni
I (don't) understand	(No) Ho entenc
Do you speak English?	Parleu anglès?
Where? When?	On? Quan?
What? How much?	Què? Quant?
Here, There	Aquí, Allí/Allá
This, That	Això, Allò
Open, Closed	Obert, Tancat
With, Without	Amb, Sense
Good, Bad	Bo(na), Dolent(a)
Big, Small	Gran, Petit(a)
Cheap, Expensive	Barat(a), Car(a)
I want	Vull (pronounced "vwee")
I'd like	Voldria
Do you know?	Vostès saben?
I don't know	No sé
There is (Is there?)	Hi ha(?)
What's that?	Què és això?
Do you have…?	Té…?
Today, Tomorrow	Avui, Demà

Accommodation

Do you have a room?	Té alguna habitació?
…with two beds/ double bed	…amb dos llits/llit per dues persones
…with shower/bath	…amb dutxa/bany
It's for one person (two people)	Per a una persona (dues persones)
For one night (one week)	Per una nit (una setmana)
It's fine, how much is it?	Esta bé, quant és?
Don't you have anything cheaper?	En té de més bon preu?

Directions and transport

How do I get to…?	Per anar a…?
Left, Right, Straight on	A la dreta, A l'esquerra, Tot recte
Where is…?	On és…?
…the bus station	…l'estació de autobuses
…the train station	…l'estació
…the nearest bank	…el banc més a prop
…the post office	…l'oficina de correus
…the toilet	…la toaleta

Where does the bus to…leave from?	De on surt el autobús a…?
Is this the train for Barcelona?	Aquest tren va a Barcelona?
I'd like a (return) ticket to…	Voldria un bitlet (d'anar i tornar) a…
What time does it leave (arrive in)?	A quina hora surt (arriba a)?

Numbers

1	un(a)
2	dos (dues)
3	tres
4	quatre
5	cinc
6	sis
7	set
8	vuit
9	nou
10	deu
11	onze
12	dotze
13	tretze
14	catorze
15	quinze
16	setze
17	disset
18	divuit
19	dinou
20	vint
21	vint-i-un
30	trenta
40	quaranta
50	cinquanta
60	seixanta
70	setanta
80	vuitanta
90	novanta
100	cent
101	cent un
200	dos-cents (dues-centes)
500	cinc-cents
1000	mil

Days of the week

Monday	dilluns
Tuesday	dimarts
Wednesday	dimecres
Thursday	dijous
Friday	divendres
Saturday	dissabte
Sunday	diumenge

Menu reader

Basic words

To have breakfast	Esmorzar
To have lunch	Dinar
To have dinner	Sopar
Knife	Ganivet
Fork	Forquilla
Spoon	Cullera
Table	Taula
Bottle	Ampolla
Glass	Got
Menu	Carta
Soup	Sopa
Salad	Amanida
Hors d'oeuvres	Entremesos
Omelette	Truita
Sandwich	Entrepà
Toast	Torrades
Tapas	Tapes
Butter	Mantega
Eggs	Ous
Bread	Pa
Olives	Olives
Oil	Oli
Vinegar	Vinagre
Salt	Sal
Pepper	Pebre
Sugar	Sucre
The bill	El compte
I'm a vegetarian	Sóc vegetarià/ vegetariana

Cooking terms

Assorted	Assortit
Baked	Al forn
Char-grilled	A la brasa
Fresh	Fresc
Fried	Fregit
Fried in batter	A la romana
Garlic mayonnaise	All i oli
Grilled	A la plantxa
Pickled	En escabetx
Roast	Rostit
Sauce	Salsa
Sautéed	Saltat
Scrambled	Remenat
Seasonal	Del temps
Smoked	Fumat
Spit-roasted	A l'ast
Stewed	Guisat
Steamed	Al vapor
Stuffed	Farcit

Fish and seafood/Peix i marisc

Anchovies	Anxoves/Seitons
Baby squid	Calamarsets
Clams	Cloïses
Crab	Cranc
Cuttlefish	Sipia
Hake	Lluç
Lobster	Llagosta
Monkfish	Rap
Mussels	Musclos
Octopus	Pop
Prawns	Gambes
Razor clams	Navalles
Salmon	Salmó
Salt cod	Bacallà
Sardines	Sardines
Sea bass	Llobarro
Sole	Llenguado
Squid	Calamars
Swordfish	Peix espasa
Tuna	Tonyina

Meat and poultry/Carn i aviram

Charcuterie	Embotits
Chicken	Pollastre
Chorizo sausage	Xoriço
Cured ham	Pernil serrà
Cured pork sausage	Llonganissa
Cutlets/chops	Costelles
Duck	Ànec
Ham	Pernil dolç
Lamb	Xai/Be
Liver	Fetge
Loin of pork	Llom
Meatballs	Mandonguilles
Pork	Porc
Rabbit	Conill
Sausages	Salsitxes
Snails	Cargols
Steak	Bistec

Vegetables/Verdures i llegums

Artichokes	Carxofes
Aubergine/eggplant	Albergínia
Broad/lima beans	Faves
Chickpeas	Cigrons
Courgette/zucchini	Carbassó
Garlic	All
Haricot beans	Mongetes
Lentils	Llenties

Mushrooms	Xampinyons
Onions	Cebes
Potatoes	Patates
Spinach	Espinacs
Tomatoes	Tomàquets
Wild mushrooms	Bolets

Fruit/Fruita

Apple	Poma
Banana	Plàtan
Grapes	Raïm
Melon	Meló
Orange	Taronja
Pear	Pera
Strawberries	Maduixes

Desserts/Postres

Cake	Pastís
Cheese	Formatge
Fruit salad	Macedonia
Crème caramel	Flam
Ice cream	Gelat
Rice pudding	Arròs amb llet
Tart	Tarta
Yoghurt	Yogur

Catalan specialities

Amanida Catalana Salad served with sliced meats (sometimes cheese)

Arròs a banda Rice with seafood, the rice served separately

Arròs a la marinera Paella: rice with seafood and saffron

Arròs negre "Black rice", cooked in squid ink

Bacallà a la llauna Salt cod baked with garlic, tomato and paprika

Botifarra (amb mongetes) Grilled Catalan pork sausage (with stewed haricot beans)

Calçots Large char-grilled spring onions, eaten with romesco sauce (see below), available February/March

Canelons Cannelloni, baked pasta with ground meat and béchamel sauce

Conill all i oli Rabbit with garlic mayonnaise

Crema Catalana Crème caramel, with caramelized sugar topping

Escalivada Grilled aubergine/eggplant, pepper/capsicum and onion

Espinacs a la Catalana Spinach cooked with raisins and pine nuts

Esqueixada Salad of salt cod with peppers/capsicums, tomatoes, onions and olives, a summer dish

Estofat de vedella Veal stew

Faves a la Catalana Stewed broad beans, with bacon and *botifarra*, a regional classic

Fideuà Short, thin noodles (the width of vermicelli) served with seafood, accompanied by *all i olli*

Fuet Catalan salami

Llenties guisades Stewed lentils

Mel i mató Curd cheese and honey, a typical dessert

Pa amb tomàquet Bread (often grilled), rubbed with tomato, garlic and olive oil

Pollastre al cava Chicken with *cava* (champagne) sauce

Pollastre amb gambes Chicken with prawns

Postres de músic Cake of dried fruit and nuts

Salsa Romesco Spicy sauce (with chillis, nuts, tomato and wine), often served with grilled fish

Samfaina Ratatouille-like stew (onions, peppers/capsicum, aubergine/ eggplant, tomato), served with salt cod or chicken

Sarsuela Fish and shellfish stew

Sípia amb mandonguilles Cuttlefish with meatballs

Suquet de peix Fish and potato casserole

Xató Mixed salad of olives, salt cod, preserved tuna, anchovies and onions

Drinks

Beer	Cervesa
Wine	Vi
Champagne	Xampan/Cava
Coffee	Cafè
Espresso	Cafè sol
Large black coffee	Cafè Americà
Large white coffee	Cafè amb llet
Small white coffee	Cafè tallat
Decaf	Descafeinat
Tea	Te
Drinking chocolate	Xocolata
Crushed ice drink	Granissat
Milk	Llet
Tiger nut drink	Orxata
Water	Aigua
Mineral water	Aigua mineral
...(sparkling)	...(amb gas)
...(still)	...(sense gas)

small print & Index

A Rough Guide to Rough Guides

Barcelona DIRECTIONS is published by Rough Guides. The first *Rough Guide to Greece*, published in 1982, was a student scheme that became a publishing phenomenon. The immediate success of the book – with numerous reprints and a Thomas Cook Prize shortlisting – spawned a series that rapidly covered dozens of destinations. Rough Guides had a ready market among low-budget backpackers, but soon also acquired a much broader and older readership that relished Rough Guides' wit and inquisitiveness as much as their enthusiastic, critical approach. Everyone wants value for money, but not at any price. Rough Guides soon began supplementing the "rougher" information about hostels and low-budget listings with the kind of detail on restaurants and quality hotels that independent-minded visitors on any budget might expect, whether on business in New York or trekking in Thailand. These days the guides offer recommendations from shoestring to luxury and cover a large number of destinations around the globe, including almost every country in the Americas and Europe, more than half of Africa, and most of Asia and Australasia. Rough Guides now publish:

• Travel guides to more than 200 worldwide destinations
• Dictionary phrasebooks to 22 major languages
• Maps printed on rip-proof and waterproof Polyart™ paper
• Music guides running the gamut from Opera to Elvis
• Reference books on topics as diverse as the Weather and Shakespeare
• World Music CDs in association with World Music Network

Visit **www.roughguides.com** to see our latest publications.

Publishing information

This 1st edition published February 2005 by **Rough Guides Ltd**, 80 Strand, London WC2R 0RL. 345 Hudson St, 4th Floor, New York, NY 10014, USA.

Distributed by the Penguin Group
Penguin Books Ltd, 80 Strand, London WC2R 0RL
Penguin Group (USA), 375 Hudson St, NY 10014, USA
Penguin Group (Australia), 487 Maroondah Highway, PO Box 257, Ringwood, Victoria 3134, Australia
Penguin Group (Canada), 10 Alcorn Avenue, Toronto, ON M4V 1E4, Canada
Penguin Group (NZ), 182–190 Wairau Road, Auckland 10, New Zealand
Typeset in Bembo and Helvetica to an original design by Henry Iles.
Printed in China.

208pp includes index
A catalogue record for this book is available from the British Library.

ISBN 1-84353-395-2

Help us update

We've gone to a lot of effort to ensure that the first edition of **Barcelona DIRECTIONS** is accurate and up-to-date. However, things change – places get "discovered", opening hours are notoriously fickle, restaurants and rooms raise prices or lower standards. If you feel we've got it wrong or left something out, we'd like to know, and if you can remember the address, the price, the phone number, so much the better.

We'll credit all contributions, and send a copy of the next edition (or any other DIRECTIONS guide or Rough Guide if you prefer) for the best letters. Everyone who writes to us and isn't already a subscriber will receive a copy of our full-colour thrice-yearly newsletter. Please mark letters: "**Barcelona DIRECTIONS Update**" and send to: Rough Guides, 80 Strand, London WC2R 0RL, or Rough Guides, 4th Floor, 345 Hudson St, New York, NY 10014. Or send an email to **mail@roughguides.com**.

Have your questions answered and tell others about your trip at **www.roughguides.atinfopop.com**.

Rough Guide credits

Text editor: Claire Saunders
Layout: Dan May
Photography: Ian Aitken
Cartography: Jasbir Sandhu
Picture editor: Jj Luck

Proofreaders: Ken Bell, Diane Margolis, Nikky Twyman
Production: Julia Bovis
Design: Henry Iles
Cover art direction: Louise Boulton

The author

Jules Brown first visited Barcelona in 1985. Apart from this book he has also written half-a-dozen other Rough Guides, and contributed as researcher to and editor of many others. But he's beginning to think he's left it too late to play for Huddersfield Town.

Photo credits

All images © Rough Guides except the following:

Front cover La Pedrera © Robert Harding
Back cover Cable car © Alamy
pp.9 & 10 Sagrada Família © Dorling Kindersley
p.14 Hotel Neri © Hotel Neri
p.15 Prestige © Prestige
p.15 Arts Barcelona © Immanol Sisitiaga for Absolute Visual
p.15 Grand Marina © Jordi Llobet
p.15 Claris © Mr. Martin Nocholas Kunz
p.18 Dia de Sant Jordi © Pat Behnke/Alamy
p.19 Human Audio Sponge performing at the Sónar festival © Advanced Music

p.19 Festa de la Mercè © AA World Travel Library/Alamy
p.19 Human Pyramid © Gregor Schmid/Corbis
p.19 Fira de Santa Llúcia © Heidi Grassleu/Dorling Kindersley
p.33 Museum of Textiles © Peter Aprahamian/Corbis
p.42 Gran Teatre del Liceu © Alan Keohane/Dorling Kindersley
p.95 Museum of Textiles © Peter Aprahamian/Corbis

Index

Map entries are marked in colour

INDEX

INDEX